Connecticut Valley Vernacular

Connecticut Valley Vernacular

The Vanishing Landscape and Architecture of
the New England Tobacco Fields

James F. O'Gorman

With photographs by Jack Delano, Lewis W. Hine,
The Howes Brothers, Jerome Liebling, Cervin Robinson, and the author

UNIVERSITY OF PENNSYLVANIA PRESS

Philadelphia

Publication of this volume was assisted by grants from
Wellesley College and Furthermore, the publication
program of the J. M. Kaplan Fund

10 9 8 7 6 5 4 3 2 1

Published by
University of Pennsylvania Press
Philadelphia, Pennsylvania 19104-4011

Text Design by George Lang

Library of Congress Cataloging-in-Publication Data
O'Gorman, James F.
   Connecticut valley vernacular : the vanishing landscape
and architecture of the New England tobacco fields /
James F. O'Gorman with photographs by Jack
Delano . . . [et al.].
      p.   cm.
   ISBN 0-8122-3670-X (cloth : alk. paper)
   Includes bibliographical references (p.) and index
   1. Tobacco—Connecticut River Valley. 2. Vernacular
architecture—Connecticut River Valley. 3. Connecticut
River Valley—Social life and customs. I. Title
SB273.O46   2002
633.7'1'0974—dc21   2002020333

FRONTISPIECE. Landscape, people, and architecture:
field workers, American Sumatra Company, Connecticut,
1917. Men and boys begin to harvest a vast field of outdoor plants while a row of curing sheds with horizontal
vents waits in the distance. The superintendent told the
photographer that they "hire boys because we can't get
men to do the work." These youngsters ranged in age
from nine to fifteen years; many of them lived in Hartford and rode the trolley to and from the fields. (Lewis
W. Hine for the National Child Labor Committee. Courtesy Photography Collections, University of Maryland,
Baltimore County)

To Susan Danly, and the Meadow Road menagerie

CONTENTS

ILLUSTRATIONS

Introduction

We live in an era of Clorox-bottle boats and beer-can cars, far removed from the sensual world of natural materials, hard labor, or pungent smells. Post industrial men and women have their ears plugged with cell phones or Walkmans, their eyes glued to TVs or PCs, their noses numbed by chemical air freshener. They are in the latest stages of a process in which their senses are dulled and their attention has shifted from the actual to the artificial or the virtual. Little by little the gap grows larger and larger between people and their roots. Western life now plays out far from its origins in nature and history. Think of this essay as a pause in that on-rushing existence. This is a glance back: a study in celebration of the real, of the environmental history of one aspect, one passing phase, of the agriculture and architecture of the Connecticut River Valley.

At the legal speed limit you can drive the eighty miles between Middletown, Connecticut, and Greenfield, Massachusetts, nonstop on Interstate 91, in a little over an hour and a quarter, but to race through this part of the Connecticut River Valley on such a path at such a speed is to miss a landscape of uncommon interest. The Eisenhower interstate highway system was created at the height of the Cold War on the model of the ancient Roman roads, as a means to move people and machines (or, in time of war, men and matériel) as quickly as possible from one point to another without regard for the journey itself. As the driver on this trip you will see little but the blocky backs of long-haul eighteen wheelers and the catchy bumper stickers of SUVs lumbering between Manhattan apartments and Vermont vacation houses, but even as a passenger you will perceive all too briefly only the larger features of one of New England's more special stretches of terrain. You will skirt or slice through the centers of Hartford, Springfield, and Northampton, occasionally glimpse the snaking Connecticut River as it crosses beneath the six-lane pavement, view in passing Mount Tom and the Holyoke Range near Northampton, and Mount Toby and Mount Sugarloaf at Sunderland and South Deerfield, whiz by shopping malls, commercial strips, subdivisions, and light industrial buildings, and, perhaps, even catch sight of the odd bit of agriculture seen through forested frames. But you will miss the key to the territory.

Detour down an off-ramp and you will begin to experience the details of this extraordinary, fast-changing landscape. Once off the Interstate you will find the remnants of historic towns dotted with neoclassical houses and white-painted churches; climb the steep slopes of isolated hills for aerial views over the river; and, in season, stop to buy newly boiled maple syrup at steaming sugar shacks, bag freshly picked vegetables at the many family-owned roadside farm stands, or quaff ready-pressed cider at upland orchards. Many of these things you can encounter in other parts of New England, but one thing sets the lower Connecticut Valley off from the rest of the region. What is remarkable to most travelers who take the time to wander through this landscape is a surprising crop growing in the summer fields. This is tobacco country.

We usually associate tobacco with cigarettes and the South, but if you drive along the river roads of Windsor, Connecticut, or Hatfield, Massachusetts, in season you will see dotting the old agricultural landscape occasional dark green patches of exposed broadleaf or rectangular stretches of white tenting covering shade-grown tobacco. This crop is intermingled with fields of corn, potatoes, cucumbers, strawberries, and pumpkins, as well as historic buildings, sprawling housing developments, shopping centers, commercial strips, and high-tech industries. This is the specialty of the region; this is cigar-leaf tobacco.

Unlike food crops, tobacco is not just picked and sent to market; it must be seasoned first. Year round you will notice beside those fields the long, relatively low, gabled wooden barns (locally they are usually called "sheds") built for curing tobacco (Plate 1). The leaf has been grown in the Valley since precolonial days; this special building type has existed for a little more than one hundred and fifty years. The sheds are still numerous, but there were many more three-quarters of a century ago. Where you see one today there may once have been a dozen or more. As tobacco production dwindles, these structures are often abandoned, to vanish because of fire or collapse (or they are pulled down for their old chestnut timbers, which are then converted into furniture). Yet, although their ranks have been thinned and they have been elbowed aside by changing social and economic patterns, tobacco sheds remain the most characteristic example of agricultural vernacular architecture in the Connecticut River Valley. Tobacco itself survives as an attractive cash crop for some of today's small farmers as well as for the few remaining corporate growers, though its acreage decreases a little more each year in the wake of the introduction of homogenized sheet wrapper in the 1950s, the Surgeon General's report on smoking in the 1960s, and the vicissitudes of the market since.

We may not lament the slow passing of tobacco in American life, but that is no reason not to recognize the role the weed played in the environmental and social history of the western parts of Connecticut and Massachusetts or the architectural type that remains—at least for awhile—the visible sign of that history.

These tobacco sheds are the common relics of a vanishing episode of Valley life. They remind us of an era in which a majority of New Englanders lived closer to the timetable of the seasons. This was "a calendar based on sowing and harvesting," as Mary Taylor Simeti wrote about life in another agricultural area, "on death and rebirth, [that] is irrelevant to us now, its recurrent cycles out of step with the linear conception of time and progress that urges us forward." The sheds in season harbor not vital sustenance but intoxicating pleasure—one that is quickly going out of fashion. They are nonetheless—in construction and content—physical manifestations of people's adapting nature to their own use, of shifting immigrant populations, of long hot hours laboring in the summer fields, of the autumnal curing process, and of a fading way of life. As we know from nineteenth-century agricultural diaries, life once depended on a close familiarity with soil, husbandry, plant life, and climate. Diary entries habitually begin with observations about the weather. Daily activities in the United States now

largely unfold far from the land, but in parts of the Connecticut River Valley signs of an earlier era, of a life that reverberated with the seasons, linger just a little longer. In what follows I briefly outline the formation and transformation of the Connecticut Lowlands, the tides of people who have worked the fields, and the architecture of the Valley's characteristic building types, including the wooden curing sheds, stripping rooms, and textile shade tents. This book is an attempt to capture something of the environmental and historical aura of the New England tobacco fields before they completely disappear.

For years I wondered about those long windowless gabled structures in the fields bordering the highway as I sped between Boston and New York. I knew they were not covered bridges because there were no streams flowing beneath them although the two structures (which incidentally began to appear at about the same time in the early nineteenth century) look a lot alike from a distance, especially when the wagon doors are open on the ends of the sheds. It was not until I settled into the Valley that I took the time, to quote folklorist Henry Glassie, "to crack them open and learn their meanings." During the height of the season I moved into a house on a river road near the top of the tobacco growing area, and when my neighbors began to harvest their crop and hang it in their sheds I had what can only be described as an aesthetic jolt. An aesthetic jolt? These are mere utility sheds, created without any conscious pretense to architectural distinction; how could they call forth such a reaction?

These long solid gabled forms echo the flat fields they define (see Frontispiece). They become light airy structures in late summer as their open ventilators allow the flow of breezes so necessary to the curing of the leaves that are hung within (Plate 2). The transformation gives rise to an open, picturesque form etched by sunlight and shadow. When I first encountered this transformation I was reminded of an aphorism in a talk delivered in 1877 by Henry Fowle Durant, the founder of Wellesley College, where I teach. "All beauty is the flower of use," he said, reiterating a principal view of New England transcendentalism. Here is a building that responds economically and therefore beautifully to one specific need. Here is a test-tube example of that succinct and never-improved-upon definition of architecture by the ancient Roman Vitruvius, who wrote that it is the confluence of utility, structure, and beauty (*Utilitas, Firmitas, Venustas*). Here is a building type shaped by need that grows more beautiful with use and age. Here is a vernacular form that has received no sustained discussion in print. Here was a vital architectural image whose meaning I wanted to explore.

It would never do, however, to focus narrowly on the sheds or tents. To study architecture, or, more broadly, the artifacts of material culture, means to study the geographical, eco-nomic, and social conditions they reflect. These buildings cannot be understood divorced from the broader context that includes the peculiarities of the landscape upon which they stand and the ranks of people who erected or filled them. The sheds exist as the result of forces that began in prehistoric time, forces that produced in the Valley the perfect combination of soil and climate that makes it suitable for growing cigar-leaf tobacco. They are also the result of historical forces, forces that brought wave after wave of native and immigrant peoples to farm the rich fields of the lower Valley. And, finally, they are the result of technological forces, of evolving agriculture and the design of a traditional farm structure adapted for a divergent use. Since these various forces account for the character of the Connecticut Valley environment between the middle of the nineteenth and the middle of the twentieth centuries, they will form the background to my discussion of the rise of the Connecticut Valley tobacco shed during that period.

The recent geological history of the region has produced a landscape well adapted to agricultural abundance and a climate made for growing what was called in the eighteenth century "Indian weede." A glance at a topographical map of the Connecticut River will show that it flows in a relatively narrow valley from its source near the Canadian border to just above the Massachusetts state line, and then broadens into a wide alluvial plain with meadows (in New England usage, "intervales") running along both its banks. This is the Connecticut Valley Lowland, and here, on a stretch that reaches from just above Greenfield to just above Middletown, the dominance of tobacco as a cash crop rose and fell from a decade or two before 1850 to sometime after 1950. (A subsidiary area of cultivation existed in the Housatonic Valley to the west.) In this region the river wanders through an ancient glacial lakebed, and the sedimentation left as the water receded is ideal for agriculture when it is well fertilized. The growing season in this latitude is moist and short. This suits the cultivation of tobacco, a weed that can spring from a minuscule seed into an eight- or ten-foot plant in a couple of months, producing generous leaves destined to become the makings of the finest cigars. Along the river-banks in summer stretched the vast fields of broadleaf tobacco, large, velvety, dark-green leaves that gave a special character to the Valley floor. After 1900, acres of white tents intermingled with these exposed fields, providing shade for growing top quality cigar wrappers and adding a unique aspect to the river edges.

The cultivation of tobacco is a high risk, labor intensive, controversial, but potentially very rewarding occupation for owners if not for laborers. Cultivation demands constant attention, backbreaking handwork in the fields and under the tents, and knowledgeable adherence to detail in the curing sheds and stripping and sorting rooms. Its history in the Valley is one of close

relationship between people and land. In briefly outlining the history of tobacco people in the Valley I am aware of and have tried to narrow what the late Amherst College professor Theodore Baird thought of as the wide gap between "the simplification of language" and "the unutterable complexity of being alive." I have thought it best to permit the people who worked the weed, built the sheds, and erected the tents to speak for themselves as much as possible. I have stayed close to original and meaningful secondary sources, drawing upon quotations from oral histories, interviews, agricultural diaries, local histories, newspapers, and even novels. I have employed these verbal sources as aids to crack the meaning of this vernacular environment, but it is ultimately the shed or the shade tent itself that bears primary witness to the history of tobacco cultivation. And I present a brief overview rather than an extensive inventory, one heavily weighted toward the nineteenth and early twentieth centuries.

Among the primary written sources for the study of the New England tobacco fields, I was surprised to find the humble agricultural diary to be the most useful and the most touching. Such a diary is usually tiny, often laconic, characteristically difficult to decipher, frequently primarily devoted to repetitious recordings of temperature and weather conditions. But it brings the modern researcher as close to the daily life of the nineteenth-century Valley farmer as it is possible to get—to his concerns about his family, land, crop planning, building construction and repair, and other quotidian chores. Turning page after page of these fading mementos of a lost way of life, reading with squinting eyes the brief, closely repetitious entries, animates the past in the same way that flipping the pages of a book of slightly different drawings sets them in motion. Next to studying vintage photographs (Figure 1) it is the most direct way of reanimating the historical agricultural landscape.

In the nineteenth century that landscape was owned by Yankee descendants of the pioneers. At the end of the century the combination of played-out farms, opportunities elsewhere (in the city or the West), and influx of immigrants saw that land gradually change hands from the old Yankees to Slavic newcomers. Within a generation the single-minded "Polanders" had revitalized the agriculture of the tobacco fields and become the dominant ethnic and economic presence in the area. They in turn hired later migrants and immigrants.

The newly revived family-owned farms helped to produce some of the leaf demanded by a expanding market for cigars around 1900, but another development really gave the local tobacco economy a shot in the arm. Experiments with growing Sumatra seed under shade proved that the Valley could compete in the world market for fine cigar leaf. "Shade-grown" produced a crop well suited to cigar wrappers, while the older broadleaf and Connecticut seed, or "outdoor," tobaccos were now best suited for filler and binder. This new cultivation required the erection of acres of cheesecloth "tents" covering the growing plants, and changed the way leaf was harvested and hung for curing. It also changed the look of the landscape. Parts of the intervales were now transformed into broad architectural acres marked in summer by rectangles of white cloth, beneath which the delicate leaves grew to maturity (see Figure 7 below). Where earlier the individual farmer and a couple of hands had planted a few acres of broadleaf, these vast fields of textile architecture were owned or contracted for by large corporations that sprang up to produce Valley leaf in vast quantities. And they employed armies of men, women, and children to work in the fields and in the sheds. Among them came migrant and immigrant workers, including southern blacks as well as Puerto Ricans, Jamaicans, and other West Indians who first arrived during the labor shortage of World War II (when the government thought of tobacco as an essential crop!). The labor force over time has proven to be a microcosm of immigration history, and the tobacco fields were (and remain) equal opportunity workplaces.

The number of sheds increased under these forces. The Connecticut Valley tobacco barn, or "hanging house," is a regional variation of that used in other tobacco-growing areas and is recognized as such by recent scholarship. The Valley

FIGURE 1. All hands, including men, boys, and one girl, pitch in at harvest time about 1900. Broadleaf stalks have been chopped and laid on the ground to wilt. They will be speared onto the laths in the holder behind the boy, then hauled to the shed in the background. There the vent boards have been thrown open on their side hinges to begin the drying process. (Photo: Howes Brothers. Courtesy Ashfield Historical Society)

shed developed during the middle of the nineteenth century out of the old three-bay English barn. It might have been built by the farmer himself or—especially in the twentieth century—by professional builders for the corporations. It is a structure in which a series of transverse frames are erected as the armature of the building and the rack upon which to hang the tobacco, then covered with gable roofing and board siding. There is a direct relationship between the number of acres of tobacco harvested and the shed capacity required. Capacity can be achieved by the number of sheds, the length and width of the individual shed, or both.

Local tobacco is cured by air. Drying is accomplished by ventilation produced by adjustable openings along the sides of the sheds, in the gables, and at the roof ridge. Once the type was established it changed little (although the sharp eye on close inspection will find small variations among Valley sheds). The sheds stand closed for most of the year, but with vents open during the fall curing season, they are thin, flexible structures lending their own special presence to the characteristic Valley landscape. They represent the harnessing of natural elements to human desires, the toil of countless individuals, and, when full of drying tobacco, money in the bank (Plate 3).

The curing sheds and sorting houses of the Connecticut River Valley are not the only building types associated with the history of the tobacco industry, but they are the only ones that formed part of the agricultural landscape. Tobacco warehouses existed in the towns, and the large corporate growers had headquarters in Hartford and other cities. When the tobacco leaves have been sold, packed, and shipped, I lose interest in them. My focus is on the architecture of the tobacco fields.

The profile of the tobacco environment of the Connecticut River Valley could be drawn from any number of points of view: those of the farmer, agronomist, experimental researcher, shed builder, migrant field worker, leaf sorter or packer, leaf buyer, cigar maker, cigar company executive, tobacco lobbyist, smoker, or anti-tobacco crusader. I write as an historian of architecture who has surveyed most of these angles. I look at this subject as a disinterested scholar. My approach views architectural history in its broadest terms. It assumes that the history of the land and the people are important to understanding the meaning of the sheds. It also assumes that the gabled sheds and boxy tents constitute architecture worth writing about. This essay flows from a statement written by one of America's most celebrated architects, Frank Lloyd Wright: "folk-structures . . . are of the soil. Though often slight, their virtue is intimately related to environment and to the heart-life of the people. Functions are usually truthfully conceived and rendered invariably with natural feeling. Results are often beautiful and always instructive." Connecticut River tobacco sheds are rooted in the natural and human histories of the Valley, reflect in their forms one specific agricultural endeavor, and attract us by their time-enhanced beauty.

The following summarizes extensive though hardly exhaustive research in the field and in the library. It is aimed at a general audience. Scholars and others who seek more depth will find the list of further reading, while not comprehensive, a reasonable starting point for their own excursions into the history of the Valley's vernacular environment. My intention is valedictory. The text and—perhaps more important—the selected photographs, some vintage and some taken specifically for this book, are intended to record and celebrate the vernacular architectural history—the landscape, people, and buildings—of this vanishing way of life.

FIGURE 2. Thomas Cole's famous 1836 painting, *View from Mount Holyoke, Northampton, Massachusetts, after a Thunderstorm (The Oxbow)*, depicts the topography of the Connecticut River Valley just at the moment local farmers began to turn to commercial tobacco cultivation. Flanked by mountains on either side of the meandering river, the intervale slices diagonally across the canvas from lower right across the oxbow and into the storm. "The fields upon the margin [of the river]," wrote Cole, "have the richest verdure." They were soon to be spread with the shiny dark green of cigar-leaf tobacco. (The Metropolitan Museum of Art, New York, gift of Mrs. Russell Sage, 1808)

Tobacco Fields
The Connecticut Intervales

The Connecticut River rises in a series of lakes near the Canadian border in northern New Hampshire, falls some 1,600 feet in the course of its more than four-hundred-mile journey, and empties into Long Island Sound between Old Saybrook and Old Lyme, Connecticut, having drained more than 13,000 square miles. It separates the states of Vermont and New Hampshire, cuts Massachusetts into western one-third and eastern two-thirds, and nearly bisects Connecticut. "Sweet and winsome," in the words of Edwin Bacon, "rather than proud and majestic" like the Hudson River to the west (which flows for only three-quarters of the Connecticut's length), the Connecticut has nonetheless played a major role in the economic and cultural life of New England.

The Connecticut River Valley is relatively narrow until it nears the northern state line of Massachusetts. From there the river begins to meander across lowlands between eastern and western uplands leading to the Worcester Highlands and the Berkshire Hills. The Valley here forms an elongated oval shape with its apex near Greenfield, its maximum east-west width of some twenty miles just above Hartford, and its nadir near New Haven. It is interrupted on the west by the long, north-south Metacomet Ridge through which the river breaks in Massachusetts and from which it veers eastward below Middletown, where the river and the Valley part company as the river reaches its tidal estuary at Long Island Sound.

The Valley floor to either side of the river is defined by gentle rises, "often a series of low, step-like terraces, [reaching] to the sharper slopes of bordering upland." The lowest steps contain the flat, freshwater meadows lining both sides of the river. These meadows, which the old New Englanders called intervales, are the tobacco fields (Plate 4).

The Valley profile spreads outward from riverbed to flood plain to "splendid terraces rising between intervening glens," to the highlands enclosing the Valley, again according to Edwin Bacon. The most conspicuous characteristic of this landscape, other than the hills that occasionally cut into it, is the "frequency and magnitude of the fertile meadows or intervals—intervales of common speech,—off-spreading from the River sides." Novelist Edna Ferber wrote that in Connecticut there were "great areas of meadow and streams that were like English parks made to hand." "It was Kent," she continued, referring to the English county, "transported to the wilderness." A population map of New England about 1700 would show a rim of density along the eastern seaboard and a spike rising from Long Island Sound up the Connecticut Valley. The earliest Dutch and English immigrants, like the native populations before them, found the Valley, especially the lower Valley, green and welcoming in contrast to the forbidding granitic coast and hinterlands of the Massachusetts Bay Colony. Early travelers over and over again remarked about these valued fields. Samuel Peters, in his history of Connecticut of 1782, wrote that the "spacious and fertile meadow, arable, and other lands, combined with this noble river, are at once the beauty and the main support of all New England." The intervales particularly struck Timothy Dwight, the Valley-bred president of Yale University, whose *Travels in New England* (1821–22) dwells on them at some length. "Their universal fertility makes a cheerful impression on every eye," he wrote. They are "everywhere covered with a verdure peculiarly rich and vivid." Thomas Cole, father of the Hudson River School of landscape

painting, echoed Dwight when he wrote that "the imagination can scarcely conceive Arcadian vales more lovely or more peaceful." The Connecticut's villages, he added, "are rural places where trees overspread every dwelling, and the fields upon the margin have the richest verdure" (Figure 2).

Those rich meadows attracted population; the pioneers followed wherever they led. As the cultural geographer Joseph Wood wrote, "Long strings of farmsteads paralleling the river formed linear settlements." The colonial villages mentioned by Cole, that had gradually spread northward from the mouth of the river during the seventeenth and eighteenth centuries, recorded in their very names their raisons d'être. This is especially true of a significant length of the lower Valley, the stretch of river from Middletown northward across Massachusetts that "had the most extensive meadows in New England" (Figure 3). From Middlefield and Westfield through Wethersfield, Bloomfield, and Enfield in Connecticut, across the state line into Massachusetts, past Longmeadow to Springfield and Northampton (known as the "Meadow City"), and on to Hatfield, Deerfield, Greenfield, and Northfield near the top of the state, town names celebrate the rich intervales, the geological basis for their existence (a few "field" names are found above the Massachusetts state line, but only a few). And "Meadow Road" must be among the most common street names in the river towns. Of importance to our story is the fact that the stretch

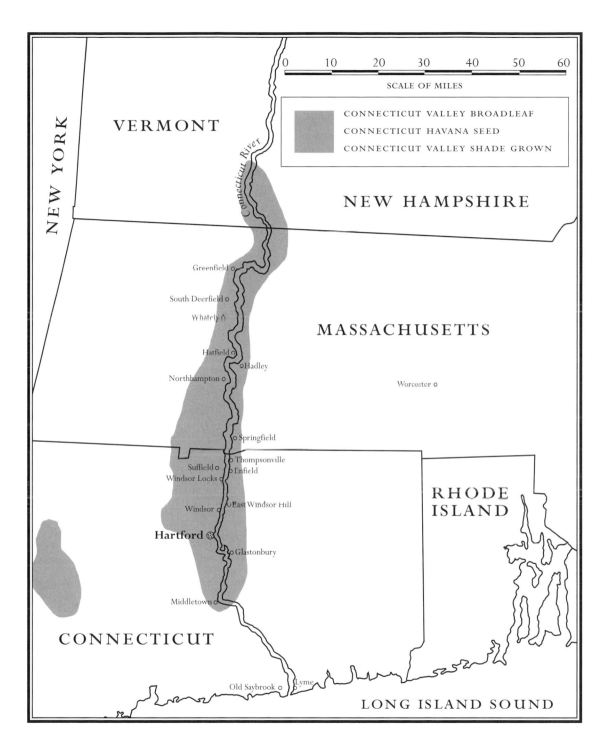

FIGURE 3. Tobacco Growing Regions of the Connecticut River Valley. The New England tobacco fields stretch along both sides of the Connecticut River from above Greenfield, Massachusetts, on the north to the vicinity of Middletown, Connecticut, on the south. On these "intervales" grew the Valley's chief crop in the late nineteenth and first half of the twentieth century. Adapted from Barakat, "New England Tobacco Barns."

between Westfield, Connecticut, and Deerfield, Massachusetts, coincides with the shape of the Valley and possesses the richest agricultural, the finest tobacco lands.

Dwight and Cole wrote of the intervales just before the wide spread of tobacco culture, but they were pointing out the rich agricultural asset that made tobacco farming such a success in coming decades. In Massachusetts and Connecticut the river flowed through the bed of glacial Lake Hitchcock, which stretched roughly from above present Middletown to above Greenfield, and whose long oval shape is left imprinted in the Valley. Its tributaries provided the "rhythmic sedimentation" which, when the lake vanished, left deep sandy-loamy soils, and beds of clay that "hold the moisture close to the surface throughout the lowland, making it available to the fields of vegetables and tobacco." Nor were there to be found in these fields the glacial boulders that plagued farmers and gave rise to the stone walls running through other parts of New England. Plowing the river meadows was almost as easy as cutting butter.

The intervales resulted from the high water table and the periodic flooding of the river. The "flow of time" in the lower Valley created optimal conditions for the growing of "Indian weede." When it is well manured the rich soil yields a bountiful harvest (Plate 5a, b). For the first centuries of occupation the colonists, like their native predecessors, grew on these rich river lands a little tobacco, along with other crops, largely for domestic consumption. By the mid-nincteenth century the intervales were increasingly planted with acres of sunlit broadleaf that slowly became the Valley's dominant cash crop.

In these years farming was not the only activity along the river. The lower Valley was the scene of major industrial development in the second half of the nineteenth and the early twentieth centuries, with mills and factories located from Hartford to Chicopee to Holyoke to Turner's Falls that produced paper, cutlery, textiles, machine tools, firearms, and shoes. But it was characteristic of that era of economic transformation that farm and factory shared the same environment, that the monuments of the industrial revolution coexisted with the traditional agricultural landscape, with fields of foodstuffs and cash crops, and with the lagging preindustrial forms of the tobacco curing sheds. The relics of that mixed nineteenth-century landscape survive to this day, with converted or abandoned brick or timber mill buildings competing for attention among the nostalgic with collapsing wooden barns, although even those signs of vanished economic prosperity are slowly disappearing.

Tobacco became the most lasting of a series of fads or "crazes" for producing cash crops that reached back to the beginning of the nineteenth century, produce that was intended to furnish the agriculturalists with hard currency in an increasingly money-oriented industrialized economy. In addition to the cultivation of potatoes, onions, cucumbers, and garden vegetables, the farmers successively sought income from lumber, then cattle, then broom corn, and, finally, tobacco. The cultivation of tobacco—cigar-leaf tobacco—became a transforming fact of the Valley landscape from the middle of the nineteenth century into the second half of the twentieth. According to one source, for example, the Valley had less than 400 acres of weed in cultivation in 1839. By the height of production in 1921 the count had risen to 31,000 acres. With the introduction of shade-grown leaf after 1900, tobacco became the most important agricultural product in the lower Valley.

What seems to be the earliest published description of the tobacco plant, in *Gerard's Herball* of 1636, captures the essence of the weed. It grows, according to this source, "in fertile and well-dunged ground seven or eight feet high, . . . [with a stalk] whereon are placed in most comely order very fair leaves, broad, smooth, and sharp-pointed . . . [with] flowers [that] grow at the top of the stalks." Add shiny dark green color to this and there you have it. Of course modern varieties differ from this seventeenth-century plant, and the flowers are now usually either pinched off to force larger leaves or bagged to capture the seed for the next planting, but en masse the overall effect of the leaf is much the same as it always has been.

Fields of tobacco have a most luxurious cast. They carpet the Valley floor. Some descriptions of the lower Connecticut Lowlands during the heyday of outdoor cultivation celebrated the lushness of the summer landscape. All along the intervales, according to Edna Ferber's description, "mile on mile, the rich green foliage stood thick as ferns in a tropical jungle" (Plate 6). But tobacco has always been a controversial crop, and there were nineteenth-century observers who loathed the sight of it. Such was the Hampshire County, Massachusetts, correspondent who asked the *New England Farmer* in 1863 "Who would have thought that this lovely valley was destined to become a tobacco growing region! That these beautiful fields were to be perverted to the production of the filthy weed!" The current attack on tobacco has a history too.

FIGURE 4. Nine- and eleven-year-old "leaf boys" at the Cybalski Tobacco Farm in Hazardville, Connecticut, September 1917. The National Child Labor Committee sent Lewis Hine to report on the exploitation of children in the tobacco fields. One superintendent told him: "We hire boys because we can't get men to do the work." A shortage of labor and the agility of the young made them desirable hands. Children have always been an integral part of the agricultural labor force. (Photo: Lewis W. Hine for the National Child Labor Committee. Courtesy Photography Collections, University of Maryland, Baltimore County)

Tobacco Leaves
Broadleaf and Shade-Grown

The cultivation of tobacco in the lower Connecticut River Valley is older than the European settlements. Its precolonial origins are well published. Although there was some trade in the weed in the colonial era, it was commonly raised for domestic consumption. It has been said that every farm had its patch of tobacco and every member of the family smoked or chewed. By the early years of the nineteenth century cigar manufacture had begun in the Valley. Cigars were originally home products made by the women in the family and peddled abroad by the farmers themselves. Larger manufacturers appear by the 1830s, turning out popular brands with names such as Supers, Windsor Particulars, and Long Nines. By that decade a few hundred acres of Connecticut were under commercial cultivation in tobacco. Experiment with Maryland seed produced a finely textured product that came to be known as Connecticut broadleaf.

The era of specialization in cigar leaf began along the river in the fourth decade of the nineteenth century. By 1845 the *Springfield Republican* noted that tobacco cultivation "has been very largely entered into in this town and vicinity within a year or two." In Whately, Massachusetts, there was one acre sown in tobacco in 1845; by 1855 there were 69 and by 1865 there were 303. In the 1840s Valley growers began to erect buildings specifically for curing their produce. By 1860 the town of Suffield, Connecticut, alone turned out sixteen million cigars worth $282,000. By 1863 the fame of the local leaf had spread as far as New Orleans, where a newspaper article on the Connecticut harvest reported that "the best tobacco for wrappers, north of Virginia, is raised in Hartford county, where the crop the present year is probably worth half a million of dollars."

We begin to find tobacco cultivation significantly mentioned during the 1840s in surviving agricultural diaries. The account book of Horace Wolcott of East Windsor, Connecticut, details his setting, hoeing, "succoring," cutting, and stripping tobacco for a number of neighboring farmers during the summer and fall of 1842. Notices of local cultivation begin to appear in the agricultural publications of this decade too. The *Cultivator* of 1844, for example, carried a letter from Henry Watson, also of East Windsor, outlining the method of raising tobacco in his area. From seedbed to curing shed the process to this day differs only in some details. There is the repetitive and never-ending annual round of starting the seed in coldframes, plowing and fertilizing the ground, transplanting or "setting" the seedlings in the spring fields; hoeing, topping (to force larger leaves), worm picking, and suckering the stalks (to remove unproductive growth) through July and August; harvesting and hanging the leaves to cure in September; and stripping, sorting, boxing, and shipping the tobacco in winter. This is all tedious handwork. Watson also announced that the Valley produced about five hundred tons of tobacco annually in two varieties, broad and narrow leaf. Broadleaf was soon to outdistance the narrow or "shoestring" variety because it was better tasting and better shaped for use as cigar wrappers.

"Tobacco like a baby," says one of the field workers in Mildred Savage's *Parrish*, a 1958 novel set in the Connecticut tobacco region. "Gotta keep it warm. Keep it sheltered. Water, hoe, sucker. All the time, care. . . . All the time work for it. Worry about it. Too hot, too wet, too dry. . . . and in the end it give you nothing but trouble." Tobacco culture has always been risky and laborious, but it held out the tantalizing but chancy possibility of high returns on investment for the individual grower (if not for his hired hands). Historian Ena Cane put it this way: "Tobacco was for the Whately [Massachusetts] farmer what racetrack and sweepstakes were to his city brother. The difference being that tobacco was a harder mistress." In the field it is subject to threats from drought, flood, wind, hail, insects, worms, blue mold and other diseases, and, in the shed, pole rot, any of which can reduce or destroy the value of the harvest. In August 1912 Solomon Terry Wells of East Windsor, Connecticut, noted that "Thunder showers with hail did a great deal of damage to the tobacco at New Milford . . . damage estimated at 80 or a hundred thousand dollars." Emil Mulnite of Connecticut, a member of a family of growers that lasted for generations, remembered one day in 1929 when four hailstorms hit the tobacco from four different directions. "That even cut off some of the stalks. There was nothing [left]. . . . You had to go for cover; you couldn't just stay out."

"Oh yes, I've been 'through the mill,'" remembered another farmer more recently. "I've had hailstones that took away all my crop and I've had fires when kids burned down three sheds. . . . I lost everything there but somehow I always came back again."

Other natural phenomena could on occasion provide more drama. Chester Woodford of Avon, Connecticut, recalled a snowstorm that hit one May. "Gee, we had a lot of tobacco, a lot of [shade] cloth, a lot of poles and wire down on the ground with snow on it." And he also remembered the flood of 1953 when water reached the eaves of a shed full of hanging tobacco. "All . . . was ruined. Just take it down and throw it away. That pert near put us out of business." But his family persevered because "they thought they could make a buck at it." Resilience, perseverance, and the optimism of the gambler are basic traits of the tobacco grower.

Even without disasters cultivation demanded constant and—especially in the era before fuel-powered machinery—backbreaking attention to the plants. In 1859 the anti-tobacco *New England Farmer* described the weed as a "disagreeable and hard crop to work. . . . The laborer must be more or less in a stooping posture, with his head in an unnatural proximity to his feet, and his face brushing the green leaves, assuming the characteristic attitude of a quadruped—*on all fours*—in his groveling, eager pursuit after 'filthy lucre.'" And, the correspondent continued, "if a man would grow old prematurely, let him raise tobacco, and labor in it himself."

This is only slight hyperbole. Fairly typical entries in the terse agricultural diaries that survive from the nineteenth century record the uncomfortable toil involved. On a day in August 1863, James Bancroft of South Windsor, Connecticut, plowed three and a half acres of tobacco in weather that was as "Hot as mustard." One typical day in June 1868, Samuel Wells of Deer-

field, Massachusetts, hoed an acre of tobacco in 98-degree heat "in the shade." "Very very hot," he moaned. On July 26, 1892, Alden Briggs of Hillside, South Deerfield, who was fifty-three years old, "hoed tobacco all day" in 95-degree heat (again in the shade, of which there was none out in those fields). Other areas of agriculture saw labor eased with the introduction of machinery, but the destiny of the delicate tobacco leaf as a cigar wrapper demands that it be treated gently. Some activity, such as transplanting seedlings with a mechanical tobacco setter invented in the 1880s, has been mechanized, but fields dotted with hunched-over laborers slowly moving among the leaves, hoeing, suckering, and occasionally mopping their brows under the July sun, are still to be seen in the Valley.

Cultivation is hard work, harvesting is no easier. In late August or early September the stalks of outdoor tobacco are cut and laid on the ground long enough to begin wilting the heavy leaves (Figure 5). They are then "speared," or strung along a wooden lath fitted with a reusable metal point, hung on racks mounted on carts pulled by horses or tractors, and hauled to the nearby tobacco shed. Within the sheds men and boys climb the frames like tall-ship sailors mounting the yards, and, balancing precariously on the beams and girts, hoist the cumbersome laths hand to hand, tier by tier until the shed is fully loaded (Figure 6). As we shall see, shade-grown tobacco, on the other hand, is harvested

FIGURE 6. A group of shed workers at Wetstone Farm, Vernon, Connecticut, 1917. The leaves have been sewn to laths by the women and girls and will be handed up to be hung in tiers by the men sitting on the overhead beams. Lewis Hine recorded the boys' ages as between twelve and fourteen years, and he complained that such labor was too difficult for such small bodies. (Photo: Lewis W. Hine for the National Child Labor Committee. Courtesy Photography Collection, University of Maryland, Baltimore County)

FIGURE 5. Men, boys, a girl, and a dog pause in their labor to pose for the camera, Ashfield, Massachusetts. The Howes Brothers took more than 23,000 photographs of local scenes between 1882 and 1907. They lined up the Valley and took its picture. Here broadleaf tobacco is cut on the stalk, laid on the ground to wilt, then "speared" onto wooden laths that are then carted to the curing shed for hanging. (Photo: Howes Brothers. Courtesy Ashfield Historical Society)

leaf by leaf, carried to the shed in carts or baskets, and sewn onto the laths, which are then hoisted onto the frames. Although it sounds rough-and-tumble, in either case it is in fact delicate work, since damage to any leaf will reduce or destroy its value. For the last century and a half, however, the risks and labor have seemed worth the effort to obtain the possible profits from what has been called "Indian gold."

For the last century and a half the Valley summer landscape has been marked by intervales lined with straight rows of young broadleaf tobacco plants set against the dark reddish-brown earth and gradually over the course of the hot months turning into a dense covering of deep green leaves (Plate 7). For the last hundred years or so, that agricultural view has been balanced by the occasional errant green shoot of tobacco reaching through a seam in the acres of square white cloth covering other parts of the Valley (Plate 8). Work was no more comfortable or easy under the cloth forms erected after 1900 for the cultivation of shade-grown tobacco than it was in the open fields, for the tents were intended to reproduce the heat and high humidity of the tropics.

If the cigarette was the smoke of the twentieth century, the cigar held sway in the nineteenth. If the cigarette was a democratic smoke, "an expensive cigar proclaimed the aristocrat, or the bloated plutocrat." Cigar consumption peaked in the late Victorian and Edwardian eras, when puffing on a custom-made "half Spanish" became an emblem of affluence among well-padded gentlemen (Plate 9). In this period smokers' preference changed from dark to light wrappers, produced from leaves raised from Sumatra seed grown under shade. This seed yielded thin, smooth-textured leaves that burned evenly. Indonesians cultivated their tobacco in the shadow of overhead vegetation to produce a light colored leaf. This led in the late 1890s to experiments in the Valley with growing the new tobacco variety under cotton tents that stretched across the intervales acre upon acre (Figure 7). The overhead cloth filters the intense sunlight of July while the sides keep the winds and insects at bay. Within, the plants are tied with strings to the overhead wires to insure their straight upward growth. The finest leaf is still grown on those humid tented acres. Even today, although its acreage is significantly reduced, "Connecticut shade" sets the standard of wrapper quality for fine smokes according to the recognized arbiter of these matters, the magazine *Cigar Aficionado*.

Broadleaf tobacco had been grown by small farmers on relatively restricted acreage alongside their other crops. With the introduction of shade-grown, the economics of the business and the look of the Valley changed dramatically. Shade fields represent a large financial investment. With shade-grown came the well-capitalized corporations, and large plantations devoted exclusively to tobacco.

FIGURE 7. Tariffville, Connecticut, 1936. After the introduction of shade-grown Sumatra seed about 1900, scenes such as this stretched across acres and acres of the intervale, especially in the area north of Hartford. Mildred Savage noted in her 1958 novel, *Parrish*, that "A continuous tent, propped up with posts, looked in the glaring sunlight like an endless field of tree stumps in a countryside of snow." Cultivating tobacco under shade produces a fine, light leaf that is highly prized for wrapping the finest cigars. (Courtesy Luddy/Taylor Connecticut Valley Tobacco Museum)

And they arrived in a hurry. The *Country Gentleman* announced in January 1902 the organization of the Connecticut Tobacco and Trading Company "to grow Sumatra tobacco under cheese cloth. It will buy 300 to 400 acres of land near Tariffville and grow 100 acres next season." By the end of the year the company reported a prosperous harvest, a new warehouse in Hartford, and the largest acreage under cultivation by a single owner in the Valley. Nor did it long have the field to itself. From 10,000,000 pounds of tobacco in the 1890s, overall production shot up to 45,000,000 pounds in 1921, about a fourth of it shade-grown. Such

large scale production required a large labor force and large scale shed construction.

By June 1902 S. B. Keach of Hartford County could see what was happening, and he laid it out in a letter to *Country Gentleman*. He thought growing tobacco under shade a "hazardous experiment" requiring large capital. "Syndicates would spring up like mushrooms," he predicted: "tent tobacco . . . will be grown in large tracts by companies of capitalists." He was right. It was not long before names like the Consolidated Cigar Corporation, Culbro, and the Hartman Tobacco Company became familiar throughout the Valley. To this day the traveler can see the former's fading C^C^C initials beneath the end peaks of sheds up and down the river. The Hartman Company resulted from the 1928 merger of several older growers. Capitalized at $4,000,000, it operated large plantations of shade-grown tobacco in Windsor, South Windsor, Poquonock, Hazardville, Buckland, and other sections of Connecticut. It owned packing houses and warehouses in Hazardville, Hartford, and elsewhere, and its corporate headquarters were located in the Hartman Building on State Street in the capital.

Keach goes on to describe the early method of tenting in some detail (Figure 8). The posts, he wrote, are

Set in rows 13 feet 4 inches apart each way . . . and fastened together by 2 x 4-inch scantling, nailed flat at the top of posts. . . . Scantling, 2 x 5-inch and 2 feet long, are also nailed to the outer row of posts, close to the ground. . . . The frame is also supported by 4 by 4-inch uprights, set 11 feet 10 inches apart in the rows. Wire is drawn tightly over the frame lengthwise, and also across the structure midway between each and every upright. Four one yard breadths of cheese cloth sewed together, cover the spaces. . . . The cheese cloth is fastened to the frames by laths. . . . The frame requires about 11,000 feet of lumber per each acre.

Those details differ a little from what became the standard during coming years. The squares he describes are smaller. His "scantling" has been replaced by overhead galvanized wire, and the fields are now laid out in 33-foot squares marked by 9-foot corner poles of red cedar slanting away from the tension of the cables to which are sewn the overhead and side cloth. Each acre requires 5,000 yards of cloth, 50 cedar poles, 350 pounds of wire, and 1,000 feet of twine. The squares are called "bents," and are indeed larger versions of the spaces that make up the curing sheds. The entire shaded field has a geometrical precision. There is an architectural regularity to all this, although it is as seasonal as a Bedouin encampment: the cloth is taken down or furled after the harvest, leaving only a skeleton of the poles and overhead wires, and spread again in the spring.

Each bent, covered with light-diffusing and humidity-retaining cotton or (now) synthetic mesh, encloses two square rods, and there are forty of them per acre. The number of rows of plants per bent is fixed, usually at ten, each containing twenty-seven plants. It has been estimated that on average there are eighteen mature leaves per healthy plant, giving 194,000 leaves per acre. As journalist Joel Lang wrote, there is a "mesmerizing symmetry" to tobacco growing. The layout of the fields is as regimented as a military parade ground. Since, as we shall see, there is a direct relationship between field capacity and shed capacity, growers need to have such mathematical organization in order to provide adequate

FIGURE 8. Beneath the cloth: textile architecture just after 1900. Upright poles and horizontal scantling and wire created the frame on which the cotton cloth was stretched to provide shade for growing Sumatra tobacco. Planting is about to begin, using horse-drawn "setters," each manned by a driver and two field hands. Women were usually to be found in the sheds or stripping houses, but they worked alongside the men at such busy moments in the cultivation of "Indian gold." (Photo: Howes Brothers. Courtesy Ashfield Historical Society)

provisions for curing. Such organization was also necessary in order to track worker productivity.

In 1902 Keach observed that the new method of production would require a new system of harvesting, one that would be both labor intensive and more costly. And, he added, "To suit the special requirements of the process by which shade grown tobacco is cured, new curing barns must be built, or old ones reconstructed." These corporate-owned barns tend to be larger than those of the broadleaf farmers. There are now Connecticut sheds that measure 40 by 200 feet or more on the ground and rise 40 feet in the air. They can cost well over $100,000.

The work of tending the growing plants and harvesting the individual leaves is different from but hardly less onerous than that for "outdoor" broadleaf. Broadleaf is harvested and hung on the stalk. The shade-grown tobacco harvest begins with "priming." Each leaf is picked as it becomes ripe, working from the ground up. Early on it was often harvested by boys or small men who could negotiate easily between rows of tender weed. Any jostling of the leaves will blemish them, so the picker's position had to be rigid and his movements small (see Figure 11 below). The bents were harvested every week or so, with just a few leaves taken with each pass. These were placed gently in wooden baskets, carried to the shed, sewn onto laths, and hung. Children are scarcer now, and the heavy baskets have been replaced by long runners between rows of plants,

runners that are dragged from the tents. This reduces the number of potentially damaging trips that the pickers must make between rows. The labor is hot, dirty, stiffening, and wearying. It is also numbingly repetitive.

These broad acres of flat-top tenting transformed the Valley landscape. Now that they have been reduced to a small fragment of their former extent, the vast stretches of whiteness are best preserved in the Technicolor footage shot from the air near the beginning of the 1961 movie *Parrish*. Their impact is best captured verbally, perhaps, by the similes of Mildred Savage, the author of the novel on which that movie was based: "acres and acres of land, covered with white cloth, stretched as far as the eye could see. A continuous tent, propped up with posts, looked in the glaring sunlight like an endless field of tree stumps in a countryside of snow, . . . [or] a white ocean, ending at the horizon against the harsh brilliant blue of an unbroken skyline. And in the whole white expanse there was no hint of motion, not of tree nor of man." The workers were hidden by the huge stalks of leaves beneath the cloth, under which "it was at least ten degrees hotter [than outside the tent]. The air was damp and tropical and artificial to the senses, like hothouse air, and heavy with the sharp, sweet smell of tobacco."

With the coming of shade-grown tobacco much of the Valley agricultural landscape, so recently dominated by acres of shiny green broadleaf, changed into vast stretches of flat white textile architecture. Clusters of gabled wooden tobacco sheds edged both, but the combination of shed and shade along the river was distinctive to the Connecticut region. The shade-grown cigar-leaf curing sheds were minor variations on the building type that had been in use for curing broadleaf by small planters since before the middle of the nineteenth century. The shade tents were a new thing on the land. Families and farm hands cultivated and harvested the older outdoor plant. Armies of field and shed hands—young and old, black and white, native and immigrant—worked the shade-grown acres. Talk to anyone who was young in the Valley before the 1970s and as likely as not he or she will have had a summer job in tobacco. People powered the industry.

Tobacco People
Yankees, Polanders, and Jamaicans

The broadleaf and shade-grown tobacco fields of the Connecticut River Valley have been worked by a succession of peoples. The first to cultivate the weed were the native Americans, from whom the English colonists learned to farm it and use it. Before the Revolution tobacco was grown largely for home consumption, although there did exist a small but brisk foreign trade. The Connecticut General Assembly found it necessary to enact a law regulating the preparation of tobacco in the 1750s, a law that empowered surveyors and packers to reject damaged or inferior leaf intended for export. Ebenezer Grant, whose handsome mid-eighteenth-century house still stands on a terrace above the intervale at East Windsor Hill, Connecticut, shipped his and his neighbors' tobacco to the West Indies along with horses, barrels, bricks, and other produce. The descendants of such colonial gentlemen oversaw the first great expansion of tobacco production during the nineteenth century. The old Yankees held sway until they began to be replaced by immigrants at the end of the century. Some recently arrived Irish and many more Slavs took control of small-scale Valley agriculture early in the twentieth century, and Polish names still enliven phonebooks from Whately, Massachusetts, to Glastonbury, Connecticut. With growing production under shade new groups successively arrived to work for the farmers and the corporations in the fields and in the sheds, and chief among them came Southern blacks, West Indians, and Puerto Ricans. Each of these groups learned tobacco lore and continued to fill the type of

FIGURE 9. Mr. and Mrs. Andrew Lyman in front of their tobacco shed near Windsor Locks, Connecticut, September 1940. The pair are smiling here because a full tobacco shed means money in the bank. Lyman's story was a common one among the Valley's "Polanders." Born Namunous in Lithuania, he immigrated about 1900 and spent the next years slaving on established farms. By 1918 he owned his own house and twenty acres of tobacco. He prospered, especially during the boom years around World War II, but lost his farm beneath the expansion of Bradley International Airport. (Photo: Jack Delano for the Farm Security Administration. Courtesy Library of Congress)

curing shed developed in the middle of the nineteenth century.

Tobacco historian E. R. Billings provides us with a snapshot of the Yankee planter of the mid-1870s. It is admittedly a highly varnished description, but it may contain some truth in the composite and it introduces another important constituency. Billings also focuses on the top of the pecking order, the landowner enjoying the fruits of a good market more or less sustained since before the Civil War. As is so often the case we know little about the laborers in his fields. The author describes his planter as a prosperous overseer who had invested considerable capital in his business, with his chief investments (other than land) in fertilizer, labor, and sheds. His fields of green stalks were usually visible from his house, "and he loves to show to visitors the plants growing in all their luxuriance, or to sit on his piazza and call attention to their waving leaves and graceful showy tops." Few had his broad knowledge of tobacco culture. He was also "a man of large and liberal views and bestows his favors with a princely hand." "He is just the person one likes to meet, jovial and good-natured," with a "table . . . well supplied from the choicest his larder affords and he cheerfully welcomes all to its side." The "friend of the poor and the companion of the rich. . . . His attachment for home, friends, and country is as firm and strong as for the plant he cultivates." And finally, "amid all the cares and perplexities incident to life, he puffs away and as the ashes drop from his cigar meditates upon the probable future of tobacco growers and all users of the weed." Had his smoky musings permitted him to see into the far distant future, Billings's planter would have been dismayed at the present ostracism of tobacco, for he considered it "one of the greatest of all vegetable products and never tires of lauding the plant and its use. He sincerely hates all anti-tobaccoites."

The Connecticut River Valley holds in its palm the cruel historical paradox of people making a living in part by growing a product that ultimately sickens or kills. But the current crusade against the weed is not the invention of a latter-day healthier-than-thou crowd. The history of tobacco cultivation and use has been paralleled by anti-tobacco laws and lobbying. From the time "Indian weede" was introduced into Europe it was attacked by politicians and preachers alike. The colonial Calvinists repeatedly enacted laws trying to control its use. In Billings's mythical planter's day, not everyone praised the Connecticut River boom. Much to his chagrin, the anti-tobacco lobby accompanied the abolitionist and temperance movements in New England, and it published book after book during the blossoming years of the culture of Connecticut leaf tobacco. The mid-nineteenth-century production growth in the Valley occurred in the face of stern moral opposition. For a full understanding of nineteenth-century life in the New England tobacco region I must introduce both the Yankee

FIGURE 10. "Affinities of Tobacco,—Idleness, Poverty, Strong Drink, Gambling, Insanity, Death." The mid-nineteenth-century commercial development of cigar-leaf tobacco in the Connecticut Valley was accompanied by an anti-tobacco crusade that paralleled contemporary temperance and abolitionist movements. The Rev. George Trask, among others, issued tract after tract condemning the cultivation and use of the weed. According to him, the "landscape of the Connecticut Valley, which has charmed the eye of millions, has been shockingly defaced by the tobacco crop." Such rhetoric did not slow cultivation. (From Trask's 1860 *Letters on Tobacco, for American Lads*)

planter and his adversary. I must briefly recognize the conflict between the patterns of belief of the tobacco grower and those of the anti-tobacco crusader.

Some nineteenth-century arguments against the cultivation and use of tobacco have a familiar ring to our ears; others are characteristic of that era. They range from its contribution to poor health (although then as later there were those who disputed this), to the immorality of its use, to its deleterious impact upon the farm and its

relation to society as a whole. The Rev. George Trask, a reformed user, whose broadsides were issued under the name of the Anti-Tobacco Tract Depository of Fitchburg, Massachusetts, spent the years between 1848 and his death in 1875 in a one-man crusade against the evils of tobacco. Writing as "Uncle Toby," he put out books such as *Letters on Tobacco, for American Lads* (1860), aimed at discouraging young users (Figure 10). Billings's composite grower might have considered tobacco "one of the greatest of all vegetable products," but the Rev. Trask wrote on the contrary that it was "vegetable poison" on a par with arsenic or prussic acid. And he was already aware of the deleterious effects of secondary smoke.

Trask's publications originated in Massachusetts, but they had Connecticut cousins in the works of the younger Arba Lankton, a well-known Hartford popcorn dealer who joined Trask and other anti-tobacconists in combining the abstinence, abolitionist, and anti-tobacco movements of the time. The slave trade too had been profitable, but no Christian should engage in it. Rum created wealth, but it was equally harmful. "Tobacco fields and distilleries of liquid death belong in the same category," according to Trask. Like his Massachusetts counterpart Lankton crisscrossed the territory sermonizing on the evils of indulgence, published tracts and other literature, and issued an annual report from 1877 on. In that of 1888 he wrapped up one of his arguments in a flow of pithy sentences: "The use of tobacco leads to Intemperance; Intemperance leads to Sabbath-breaking; Sabbath-breaking leads to the breaking of all good laws, both of man and God, and disobedience to God, leads to punishment."

In the minds of Trask, Lankton, and their peers and followers, it was not just the use of tobacco that demoralized men. Its very cultivation was immoral as well as exhausting to the land. We have seen that the anti-tobacco journal, the *New England Farmer*, thought of the bent-over cultivator of the weed as closer to an animal than to the God in whose image he had been created. In his *Anti-Tobacco Journal* of 1861 George Trask published an "Appeal to a Deacon Who Raises Tobacco on the Banks of the Connecticut." Abandon the crop, Deacon, was his text, for it destroys your soil, your fellow man, and your Christian character. "Should God send hail, frost, or fiery foxes through your fields, and lay waste, nobody should mourn, for nobody would have lost anything of value," he wrote.

This was an era in which the American landscape was viewed as sacred. Thomas Cole's contemporary, the poet William Cullen Bryant, thought of landscape paintings such as Cole's 1836 *View from Mount Holyoke (The Oxbow)* as "acts of religion," as views of the beauty and goodness of God's creation (see Figure 2). To men such as Trask and Lankton, growing tobacco on God's green earth was akin to blasphemy. They admonished men of the cloth to preach against the cultivation of the weed. "When, oh when, will Christian pulpits in that fat valley do their duty?" Trask wondered. Their duty, of course, was to rail against the misuse of God's landscape. These crusaders believed that the "banks of the Connecticut are disgraced by the tobacco crop, and the moral character of those who raise it is suffering essential injury." (An argument from religion could be stood on its head, however. Avid cigar smoker Mark Twain, for example, writing to the Rev. Joseph H. Twitchell of Hartford in December 1870, thought that "it is turning one's back upon a kindly Providence to spurn away from us the good creature he sent to make the breath of life a *luxury* as well as a necessity, *enjoyable* as well as useful, to go & quit smoking when there ain't any sufficient excuse for it.")

The tracts of professional reformers were not the only publications that attacked the weed. Ironically, the battle was joined in the pages of almost every work that discussed tobacco cultivation. Solon Robinson's 1869 compilation of *Facts for Farmers*, for example, began its section on tobacco by asserting that it "may be said to be the parent of American slavery," both human bondage on the Southern plantations and "the slavery to its use." Articles in the *Cultivator*, *Country Gentleman*, and other leading agricultural journals frequently introduced the subject with the same negative tone. The *American Agriculturalist* for March 1857 began an article on "Hints for Tobacco Growing" by stating that it was "loth [sic] to publish any thing to promote the cultivation of a plant so deleterious and so productive to wide-spread evil as we believe tobacco to be." Having thrown this sop to its editorial conscience, it then went on to fulfill the promise of its title, one of a continuous stream of such articles it published during the years of tobacco's expanding presence in the economy of the Valley. Equivocation was the order of the day in matters of tobacco cultivation and tobacco use.

The *Cultivator* for October 1864 ran an article on the "Morality of Tobacco Raising" signed "Judge French," who we know from others sources was Henry Flagg French, New Hampshire jurist, agricultural correspondent, first president of what is now the University of Massachusetts at Amherst, and, incidentally, father of the sculptor Daniel Chester French. "Suggest this topic to any assembly, no matter whether farmers or ministers, male or female, learned or ignorant, . . . and nobody waits for his neighbor's opinion; no one stops to hear both sides, but every man is ready to decide the point at once," according to this correspondent. But the Judge himself disproved his claim, since, although he says he detested the use of tobacco, his discussion is fair minded. Without the aid of modern scientific research he could assert that "it has not been proved by any statistics, that the use of tobacco shortens human life," so, "disagreeable as the weed may be to many of us, if it brings innocent enjoyment to the thousands who use it, why should we set ourselves up against it?" "Tobacco is a real comfort to our [Union] soldiers," he added, in a statement that would be repeated during twentieth-century wars.

Judge French also reported that the trustees of the Massachusetts Agricultural College (now the University of Massachusetts at Amherst) who lived in the eastern part of the Commonwealth, when in the 1860s they came to select the site for the new institution, were overwhelmed by the amount of tobacco raised and the enormous profits obtained by local farmers. A rift occurred between the western tobacco growers who sat on the board and those from the east "who were so horror-stricken with the idea of tobacco-culture, that they would not locate the College in Amherst . . . if they believed tobacco would ever be raised on its farm." In the *Country Gentleman* of the same month another correspondent attacked the Judge's even-handed treatment of the subject, asserting that "the use of tobacco blunts the morals and manners," and Christian teaching demands of all men that they "seek a refinement of their moral sense." Or, as George Trask put it in his cautionary *Letters on Tobacco*, how can a person be a "perfect gentleman and a perfect Christian" if he uses the "filthy weed"?

Other journals joined the crusade. In 1859 the *New England Farmer*, Boston-based and editorially opposed to growing the weed, ran an article pitting tobacco against what we would now call more politically correct nutritional crops. The argument was economic, with the writer trying to establish that tobacco did not pay as well as growers assumed. The *American Agriculturalist* extended the terms of the battle during the next decade. In June 1867 it thought it a "good time for the growers to pause and consider both the moral bearings of the crop, and its influence upon other products of the farm." The journal conceded that "a large sum of money may be realized by it, from a small plot of ground. But . . . it ruins the rest of the farm, by leading the cultivator to neglect it . . . [so that] pastures

become barren, the orchard fruitless. . . . Other crops bless the farm . . . . But tobacco is a blight upon the land that raises it." Nor in the *Agriculturalist*'s opinion was the negative impact restricted to the farm, for, by occupying land that might better be devoted to nutritious crops, tobacco's "influence . . . upon the community is quite disastrous." Nonetheless, throughout these years, this journal too continued to publish instructions on raising the weed.

These voices of protest came from inside the Valley as well as outside. Local growers, like Billings's planter, certainly heard them, but they were too busy making money to heed the call of health, morality, or social responsibility. James Newton Bagg of West Springfield, presumably a grower, summed up the controversy over raising tobacco when he wrote to the *New England Farmer* in 1858 that "Some people have conscientious scruples about raising it, and class the business with gambling and rum-selling. There is room for argument on both sides of the question. One thing is sure—it pays well, and that is the chief end of all labor." For Bagg and others like him, including the growing number of tobacco cultivators, the matter was economic not religious.

Despite heated controversy and manifest hazards, growers could see money in raising tobacco, at least in good years. Despite the problems of raising the crop, the expansion of tobacco wealth was rapid after the 1840s. The mid-century boom was fueled by the rise in cigar consumption and given a boost in New England by the Civil War. The profitability noted by Judge French and others was to some extent a result of the break with the larger tobacco growing areas south of the Mason and Dixon Line. "Tobacco has risen very much in price during the last six months," wrote the *Country Gentleman* in November 1861, "and if this deplorable war continues . . . it will reach a higher figure per pound than the most inveterate . . . smoker ever dreamed of." The *Springfield Daily Republican* reported in 1873 that the 1860s had been a decade of "unparalleled prosperity" among the tobacco growers (Plate 10). "The mortgage on the farm . . . vanished like a fog before the sunshine; the old barns were pulled down and replaced by new; new houses were built and filled with spic-span furniture." Not everyone exulted in the windfall, of course. In 1863 the *New England Farmer* lamented the fact that "tobacco fever has become an epidemic, and is fast becoming a mania. It would fill your down-easter with wonder and amazement to see with what a rush we go in for getting rich on other men's sins." Nonetheless, the flow of high prices drowned out the voices calling for the proscription of tobacco culture.

But the truth has always been that tobacco sometimes rewards its growers handsomely and sometimes does not. The boom of mid-century turned to poorer times, and bad years followed good, as increased competition, overproduction, changes in taste, and the economic downturn in the wake of the Panic of 1873 led to a stagnant market. In Hadley, Massachusetts, for example, tobacco production fell from more than 830,000 pounds in 1875 to just under 550,000 pounds in 1885. It did not exceed the 1875 amount until the introduction of shade-grown leaf after 1900. As a consequence cultivated acreage shrank to the best land next to the river, and many of the Yankee farmers began to abandon the crop and, indeed, the area itself. The ones who stayed and continued to enjoy at least middling prosperity faced another kind of crisis, that caused by the drainage of labor away from the New England farms.

In a 1894 article in *Scribner's* Octave Thanet sketched one of a series of "American types"—"The Farmer in the North." Like Billings's planter he is an ideal composite, a rustic old Yankee whose people had been on the land for generations. "He lives in a pleasant, old-fashioned white house that, for its size, and its stanch building may claim the dignity of a mansion. . . . [H]e . . . works with his hands and his legs and his back as well as his head. . . . He sent all his boys to college. . . . His daughters were educated in good schools." He was not necessarily or typically a tobacco farmer, but according to Thanet he shared one characteristic with all agriculturalists in New England: his type was "fading out of our national life." His sons had abandoned New England for the South and West, and "there is no one left on the farm." No Yankees, that is, but there were others ready to take their place.

The story of large-scale immigration that began with the famine Irish at mid-century and swelled into a flood of dispossessed Eastern and Southern Europeans by its end is usually told in terms of its impact on Boston, New York, Chicago, and other cities. It was to have an equally significant imprint in agricultural areas such as the Connecticut River Valley. The incoming tide of Slavic peoples began in the 1880s, reached its peak just before World War I, and subsided during the 1920s. The Yankees usually called the newcomers "Polanders" whether they came from Russia, Austria, Hungary, Germany, Lithuania, or, indeed, Poland itself. They found work in the Chicopee factories and on the Connecticut River farms. Thus in his diary for March 1890 Solomon Terry Wells noted hiring "a Polander." These newcomers infiltrated an old Yankee society that needed their labor but was appalled by their ways. Their blighted early history in New England paralleled that of many other immigrant groups elsewhere.

The new farm workers sprang from peasant stock. They came because of oppression at home, and they were welcomed locally because they would work long hard hours for minimum wages. Since the Civil War the call of the city or western farmlands had depleted the supply of available labor in New England. Many a Yankee, like young Marshall Field of Conway, Massachusetts, had decamped for richer opportunities in Chicago and elsewhere. So the Rev. Joel Ives could write in 1905 that the "rocky farms of Connecticut and the hill towns of Massachusetts have poured out with a lavish hand for the character building of our Western Empires" (leaving, in his mind, a moral vacuum he deplored in New England). By the turn of the century the situation had become acute. As one farmer put it in 1910, "all our boys are crazy to get off to the city, and we can't stop them . . . and our girls—they go to business college." It has been said of the Slavic newcomers that their hard work and cheap wages saved the agriculture of the Valley. That same farmer put it succinctly: "Without the Poles we couldn't possibly run our farms."

Not that the Yankees did not begrudge and even fear this alien presence. The perceived decline in birthrate among Anglo-Saxon women in the United States during these years led some observers to believe that the more fecund foreigners—largely uneducated and certainly unaccustomed to the responsibilities of a political democracy—would soon take over the country. The new immigrants met with general hostility. Henry Cabot Lodge, the longtime Republican Senator from Massachusetts, spoke for many when he said in 1890 that the country was being overrun by "undesirables," by which he meant Slavs and Italians. He added that he did not intend to stand by and watch "the quality of American citizenship decline," nor would he tolerate "a system which is continually dragging down the wages of American labor by the introduction or the importation of the cheapest, lowest, and most ignorant labor of other countries."

Whatever Lodge's opinion, cheap labor was welcome in the Connecticut Valley, but that did not prevent the established farmers from treating the Polanders in appalling ways. The newcomers were met at the boats in New York by enterprising middlemen, for instance, shipped by train up to Connecticut and Massachusetts, and "sold" to the farmers. In 1911 one disgusted Yankee described a distribution of the new arrivals in the barnyard of one of these agents as "a little nearer the slave trade than anything I had experienced." And, as we shall see, at least one immigrant later spoke of himself as a slave during his early years as a Connecticut farm laborer.

All members of the immigrant family, men, women, and children, worked sunrise to sunset in the fields. As one ditty put it:

> Here under a New England sky,
> Ringed by the blue New England hills,
> Old Europe ploughs and sows and tills.

They were different, these European newcomers. Article after article, book after book, and novel after novel discussed, characterized, and at times caricatured the clash between the rooted and the transplanted. Surviving members of the homogeneous Yankee society, men like Billings's planter or Thanet's farmer, witnessed with alarm the creation of a heterogeneous community in their midst. The Rev. Ives lamented that the "Pilgrim and the Puritan have had their day." The Connecticut River Valley in the 1880s contained "possibly the most distinctive survival of early New England Puritan life," according to an article published in 1903 by Edward Kirk Titus, an editorial writer for the *Greenfield Gazette*. "Soon the descendants of the Pynchons and the Chapins were marveling at the expressionless Slavic faces . . . ; at stunted figures that bespoke grinding toil; at the masculine forms of the women, that told of field-work beside the brother and husband and domestic animal." The newcomers spoke a "heathenish" language, bred large families, seemed intemperate by Yankee standards, and worshiped at Roman Catholic churches, all characteristics designed to create suspicion in the minds of the Calvinist oldsters. Ives, who was apparently fearful of or unimpressed by the papist religion imported by the immigrants, warned that the "Gospel must reach these incoming thousands or the New England of a Christian civilization will cease to be." How were these newcomers to be integrated into WASP society, made into responsible citizens of the democracy? Henry Cabot Lodge was not the only old Yankee to worry about such matters.

And, what was worse, the newcomers slowly but steadily began to improve their lot. Polanders were industrious and thrifty: "they add to agricultural resources, take care of the land and improve it. They add to the community prosperity." It was said of the Jekanoskis of Hadley, Massachusetts, for example, that by 1924 they had "made their bit of wilderness wonderfully productive." They slowly accumulated capital and acquired by mortgage the farmland abandoned by the Yankees. Solomon Wells, who had hired "a Polander" in 1890, sent his hired man to work *for* "the Polander in tobacco" in September 1908, and in March 1914 mentions a "Polander at the Steel place," presumably referring to the Slav's takeover of an old Yankee farm.

The newcomers never totally replaced the Yankees in the Valley, of course, but between 1910 and 1930 the number of local farms owned by the native-born decreased while those owned by the foreign-born increased (Plate 11). One after another these agricultural lands passed into the hands of the newcomers, and Thanet's farmer's old federal, Greek Revival, or Victorian farmhouse was now occupied by a family of transplants and many boarders. These immigrants had an "allegiance to the land." They stayed on it, and the production of tobacco and other crops increased. Eventually the oldsters' fears began to ease as second-generation Polanders melted into the "American way."

Scholarly and popular articles, historical studies, books, and even movies have featured the uneasy coming together of the immigrants and the resident population. In general fictional accounts involving the Poles and Yankees in the Valley end harmoniously, unlike King Vidor's movie, *The Wedding Night* (1935). This portrays a love affair between Tony Barrett (Gary Cooper), a writer who lives in his ancestral home, and Manya Novak, neighboring daughter of a "stern and old fashioned Polish tobacco farmer," which ends in tragedy. The more typical dynamics of this period of transition from the old order to the new are vividly dramatized by a pair of novels, Frances Newton Symmes Allen's *The Invaders* (1913) and Edna Ferber's *American Beauty* (1931). One author, a resident of the Valley, lived through the history; the other did her homework and captured the flavor of the era.

Allen's invaders were the immigrants who settled in the neighborhood of Sunderland, Massachusetts (originally known as Swampfield and called Fernfield in the novel), a Connecticut River community across from South Deerfield that by 1909, it is said, was one-third Polander in population. "We old families—somehow we're petered out," laments one of Allen's Yankees. The old places, "where generations of our family had worked," have been taken over by people with "outlandish names." One of the settled residents laments that it seems a shame "that the old families like the Wellings and the Hammonds and all the others are getting pushed out by the Irish and the Polanders." Dacre Welling, "the last of his race," has reached such a decadent state that he has run off to Paris to study art, leaving the family house "with a Polish washtub in the great-great-grandfather's dining room. . . . And chickens in

PLATE 1. The Connecticut Valley landscape is dotted with the architectural remains of the tobacco boom of the nineteenth and twentieth centuries. They give the Valley its distinctive look. Seen from afar the sheds all seem identical; seen up close they all possess distinctive traits. Some sheds are still curing "outdoor" or shade-grown leaf, some are converted to other uses, some are derelict and collapsing in on themselves. (Photo copyright Cervin Robinson)

PLATE 2. The Connecticut Valley tobacco shed in full autumnal display. The nearly dried broadleaf hangs from laths stacked into three and one-half tiers. Narrow slanting vents and wagon doors open the end of the two-aisle shed to the breezes that hasten the air curing process. No decorative returns, hex signs, or ridge vanes ornament these working agricultural structures, but their direct expression of purpose, weathered materials, and sunbathed open forms create a vernacular beauty peculiar to the Valley. (Photo: author)

PLATE 3. "Indian gold." This is broadleaf tobacco near the end of its hanging period, in the course of which it changes from green to golden brown. Tobacco has been grown in the Connecticut Valley since pre-colonial times. Cultivation and curing of "outdoor" tobacco in their current forms reach back a century and a half. (Photo: author)

PLATE 4. The intervale at Sunderland and South Deerfield, Massachusetts, looking south from Mt. Sugarloaf with the Holyoke Range in the distance. These flat bottomlands, "intervales" in New England parlance, characterize the Valley from here to Middletown, Connecticut. They form the basis on which generations of farmers built the rich tobacco economy of the region. To the left are a few surviving acres of white tents that cover shade-grown tobacco; across the river are fields of broadleaf and other crops. Both banks of the river were once lined with tobacco sheds. Only a few remain. (Photo copyright Cervin Robinson)

PLATE 5. The intervale at South Glastonbury, Connecticut, in late summer. Sandy/loamy soil formed by sediment deposited by glacial Lake Hitchcock makes these broad, flat fields, when well fertilized, highly productive farmlands. They lie just above the level of the river that defines their western boundary. In the lower view, the tobacco has been harvested and is curing in the sheds in the right distance. Other crops await their own picking. (Photos copyright Cervin Robinson)

PLATE 6. The Valley was once carpeted in summer with the dark green, shiny broadleaf, or "outdoor," tobacco, and in some areas there is still significant if ever dwindling acreage in cultivation. The leaves are fat and the harvest imminent on this farm, where the ventilation doors in the sheds have been opened in anticipation of hanging time. The towers of the University of Massachusetts at Amherst rise above the trees in the distance. (Photo copyright Cervin Robinson)

PLATE 7. Broadleaf tobacco field, Hadley, Massachusetts, 1984. Tobacco grows like a weed but nonetheless requires constant attention. Hoeing, suckering, and topping are the chief activities, all performed over long hours, beneath the hot sun for broadleaf, or in the close humidity of the tents for shade-grown. Tobacco has always been a high risk, labor-intensive, controversial, and expensive crop, easily ruined by mold or hail, with its value subject to the vicissitudes of an inconstant market. Over the last hundred and fifty years Valley farmers have been willing to take the risk in the hope of a high return on investment. In today's climate of opinion the crop has begun to lose its attraction. (Photo copyright Jerome Liebling)

PLATE 8. Shade-grown tobacco on the intervale at Sunderland, Massachusetts, with Mt. Sugarloaf in the distance. The cedar poles lean away from the tension of the overhead wire and are guyed to the ground. The side curtains are furled here, as the harvesting of the lower leaves has already begun. "Indian weede" begins as a tiny seed but springs to a height of eight to ten feet in an average of just two months. The vast acreage of tenting that marked the Valley in the early twentieth century has greatly declined. (Photo copyright Cervin Robinson)

PLATE 9. In the Victorian and Edwardian eras a fine cigar was the sign of affluence and social position among men. This image of about 1902 depicts a group of Chicago plutocrats enjoying their after supper pleasures: cigars and champagne. The gentlemen gathered here are identified as George M. Pullman of sleeping car fame, Levi Leiter, erstwhile partner of Marshall Field, Lyman Gage, a banker, P. D. Armour, the meat-packer, and John D. Rockefeller. This was the ultimate destination of the leaves grown at such hazard and sweat in the Connecticut River Valley. (Photo courtesy of Mary Alice Molloy)

PLATE 10. Whately, Massachusetts, 1985. A lonely tobacco barn sits in back of this mid-nineteenth-century house. Such remnants of the past emphasize the recent decline in tobacco production. The weed that created the quality of life represented by this house has been replaced by the hay that grows right up to the door of the shed, but here at least the old landscape is otherwise preserved. In other areas shiny glass business boxes or chipboard housing estates have spread like kudzu over the former tobacco fields. (Photo copyright Jerome Liebling)

PLATE 12. An isolated shed on the intervale at Sunderland, Massachusetts, with Mt. Sugarloaf across the river in the background. Nineteenth-century anti-tobacco crusaders thought that growing tobacco on God's earth was blasphemous. "The banks of the Connecticut are disgraced by the tobacco crop, and the moral character of those who raise it is suffering essential injury," wrote George Trask in 1862. Nonetheless, these years saw a boom in tobacco cultivation in the Valley. (Photo copyright Cervin Robinson)

PLATE 11. Smiarowski Farm on the intervale in Montague, Massachusetts, established in 1923. "Thicker and more thickly the Polish farmers spread over the valley . . . and the region bloomed like a garden. . . . Fields thick with tobacco, barns bursting with hay, silos oozing ensilage, cattle in the meadows; children and chickens and geese and dogs shouting, cackling, barking, squawking in the yard—that was a Polish farmhouse," so Edna Ferber described these places in 1931 in *American Beauty*. Tobacco sheds encompass the house. The river is just this side of the middle-distance hills. (Photo copyright Cervin Robinson)

PLATE 13. The skeleton of a two-aisle tobacco shed stands abandoned in a field by the river. With its walling removed, the structure is readily apparent: a series of transverse frames lined up to create a series of double bays called "bents." This is an "eight-bent" barn, so it could cure three to four acres of leaf. The frames are supported longitudinally by girts and diagonal bracing. Without its sheathing the fundamental flimsiness of the shed is readily apparent. (Photo copyright Jerome Liebling)

PLATE 14. Interior of a two-aisle tobacco shed on a small farm during hanging time. The leaves are hung from laths resting on beams that in turn span the transverse members of the frames. Twentieth-century frames are typically composed of posts on concrete footings, girders, and diagonal bracing in a number of different patterns. The dirt floor is standard. The end doors are open to receive the leaf-laden wagons; the vertical side vents are open to begin the curing process. (Photo: author)

PLATE 15. The Elisha Wells tobacco shed in Deerfield, Massachusetts, erected between 1852 and 1868, is one of the oldest datable sheds in the Valley. The interior is composed of hewn and sawn timbers fastened together using pegged mortise and tenon joints. The photo shows a side frame post, the longitudinal girts and diagonal bracing to which the sheathing is affixed, and mortises and peg holes. (The diagonal brace upper left has been pulled out of its mortise, and the transverse beam just below that has been sawn off.) This is a pre-industrial technology that survived in tobacco shed construction into the twentieth century. (Photo: author)

PLATE 16. Shed venting system, Hadley, Massachusetts, 2000. This is one of the two most common venting systems used in Connecticut Valley tobacco curing sheds. Every other board in the vertical siding is hinged to open like a narrow door, while a series of small ventilators dot the ridge. Freshly harvested leaf will be loaded into the shed by carts passing longitudinally from one end to the other. (Photo: author)

PLATE 17. A tobacco shed on the intervale in Montague, Massachusetts. As harvest time approaches in such fields of broadleaf tobacco, growers begin to open the vents and wagon doors of their curing houses in anticipation of the fall curing season. This shed has flanks of top-hinged openings and no ridge vent. (Photo: author)

PLATE 19. A pair of sheds at Suffield, Connecticut, that are still in active use. The nearer building has wagon doors running down one flank, one to each bent. The other three sides are vented using top-hinged boards. Farmers who prefer this kind of shed say it is easier to load than the more common "drive-through" sheds entered from the ends. (Photo copyright Cervin Robinson)

PLATE 18. A former tobacco shed in South Deerfield, Massachusetts, now used for storage. In this shed and others like it, the vents are horizontal rather than vertical. They were opened in unison by lifting the vertical cleats that join them together. It has been written that this kind of vent was used in curing shade-grown tobacco, but there seems to have been no hard and fast rule. This shed too lacks a ridge vent. (Photo copyright Cervin Robinson)

PLATE 20. A few remaining shed clusters, such as this one near Bradley International Airport in Windsor Locks, Connecticut, recall the glory days of tobacco cultivation in the early twentieth century. Agricultural activity is dormant in this view: the shade tenting is furled and the barns shut tight. The long, windowless, gabled form is characteristic of the Connecticut Valley tobacco barn. Corporate sheds such as these tend to be larger than those of the independent small farmers and constructed by contractors rather than the grower himself. (Photo copyright Cervin Robinson)

PLATE 21. The brick chimney and ground-level windows locate a former stripping room in the cellar of this derelict freestanding building. Peter Mokrzecky & Sons Inc. / Leaf Tobacco Growers and Dealers of Hadley, Massachusetts, located here in 1904 and eventually produced tobacco sufficient to fill twenty-one tobacco sheds. It is said that the Duke of Windsor smoked cigars made with Mokrzecky leaf, but that was in better times for this forlorn relic. (Photo copyright Cervin Robinson)

PLATE 22. Not all stripping areas were placed in a cellar. Here the chimney rising from the ground- level wing of an abandoned shed in Hadley, Massachusetts, signals the location of a former stripping room. The smallest component of this composition was a two-hole privy entered via a door from the interior of the hanging house. (Photo copyright Cervin Robinson)

PLATE 23. Shed exterior, Montague, Massachusetts. The seasons are etched on the surfaces of the old tobacco sheds in the Connecticut River Valley. Paint fades over the days, months, and years; hinges corrode; boards warp; ridges sway; eaves sag. All this adds up to what William Morris called the "rust of time," a deepening and enhancing of the structure's satisfying expression of fitness to purpose. (Photo: author)

PLATE 24. Past and present. The lone tobacco shed in the background is the lingering relic of a past economic life that is slowly succumbing to a bloated self-consciousness represented by the recently erected "McMansion" in the foreground. The largest appropriators of tobacco land have been Bradley International Airport and several shopping malls, but throughout the Valley former agricultural acreage is giving way to suburban sprawl and the Monopoly-set homes or pretentious trophy houses that accompany it. (Photo: author)

PLATE 25. One end of this former tobacco shed in Montague, Massachusetts, has been converted into a house complete with Palladian window, the ubiquitous emblem of architectural taste. The beauty of the tobacco shed derives from its formal evocation of purpose without recourse to such semiotic references. In its harnessing of the winds to cure tobacco leaf it parallels the translation of wind into power by the windmill or of wind into movement by the sailboat. (Photo copyright Cervin Robinson)

PLATE 26. This scene of an abandoned shed slowly subsiding now repeats itself the length of the Valley. A like fate probably awaits most of the region's unused sheds. (Photo copyright Cervin Robinson)

the front hall." The Wieniaskis now live there, with boarders named Somaski, Ostroski, and Polenski. But all this ill-tempered moaning is countered by another old-timer who thinks there is "no use in the world in keeping up all this prejudice against foreigners. They've come to stay and they're going to stay. . . . Goodness knows, we old families need something to start us on again." In the end Frances Allen argues for assimilation: the groups join together in marriage.

Edna Ferber's *American Beauty* is fulsomely but accurately described by one antiquarian book dealer as the "flamboyant story of the clash between a decadent New England family and the rising power of hot-blooded immigrants." The title refers to the beauty of the Connecticut River landscape, where "ridges were sheltering arms within which the fertile meadows lay, serene." The novel begins in the historical present (about 1930), with "vivid green" tobacco fields over which "there bent, not only the sturdy figures of men, but the broad, petticoated backs of women, the less bulky forms of young girls, and even the spindling shanks of children scarcely taller than the plants they tended." Out by the road their "strange names" are "painted crookedly on rural delivery boxes." "The Poles seem to have bought up a lot of the old places, don't they?" muses a young Candace Baldwin. "I must say they've done well by the farms." But her father, a man of long Yankee pedigree who left Connecticut in his youth to escape poverty, made his for-

tune in the West, and is now on a nostalgic journey into his past, takes a more jaundiced view: "Women working in the fields of New England like cattle. It's these Polacks. What right have they got in New England anyway?" Candace, the voice of the next generation, reminds him that the Puritans had grabbed the land from the Indians, while the Poles had "paid their hard-earned dollars" for it.

The bulk of the novel takes place around the turn of the twentieth century, in the era when the Slavs first arrived on the scene. Her neighbors are aghast when Judith Oakes, a descendant of the seventeenth-century Orrange Oakes who built the house she lives in, takes on a "Polack" hired man named Olszak. "Oakesfield resented the incoming Poles, though by now you found them employed on the manless farms all over this part of Connecticut, and up into Massachusetts. Here and there one of them owned a small farm, paying for it dollar by dollar. . . . Under their slavish tending the valley was taking on a second youth, blooming like a widow wooed. . . . [W]here the green was richest and most abundant there you knew that a Polish farmer labored in the fields."

Oakes Farm eventually becomes "a curious mixture . . . of Poland and New England" when the hired man marries Judith's niece and heir. Ferber too gives us assimilation. The mingling of old and new produces Orrange Olszak, a baby whose Yankee mother is unable to nurse him as could the Polish women in the neighborhood. Her dry breasts are metaphors for the Yankee condition at the turn of the century, a dying heritage that is only to be revitalized by the infusion of peasant stock. At novel's end Orrange Olszak is running the tobacco farm that now belongs to Baldwin.

These fictional accounts ring true. There are now many families in the Valley that represent the mingling of old Yankee and immigrant stock, along with a rise from peasantry to middle class. In 1940 the Farm Security Administration, a New Deal agency, sent Jack Delano to photograph farm life in Connecticut. Among his many striking pictures was one taken in September of a laughing couple, Mr. and Mrs. Andrew Lyman, standing before their full tobacco shed near Windsor Locks (see Figure 9). They are clearly pleased to have completed the labor of hanging the leaves behind them, and perhaps even happier to contemplate the fat check that will come their way as soon as they sell their crop. "Those leaves would bring money into their pockets and purses, money to ensure a calm and plenteous winter with no worry about food for themselves and for their animals. This was a land of plenty." It was Delano's mission to create images of agricultural success to balance the documents of dust-blown poverty that came from the cameras of other FSA photographers like Dorothea Lange.

Lyman was born Namunous in Lithuania about 1880 and came to this country at age twenty. A local town clerk anglicized his name. His first farm job earned him only room and board; according to his own account, he slept in the barn, ate apples, and drank raw milk. Late in life he remembered those as days of constant hunger and "spoke of young immigrants like himself as being slaves." But in America for young Lyman and his Slavic peers there was money and hope. By 1918 he had accumulated a few hundred dollars with which he bought twenty acres and an old house in Windsor Locks. He raised tobacco and a little livestock, and in winter worked in a tobacco factory to earn seed money for the next spring's planting. "There were good years and bad," his son remembered. During the boom times of World War II Lyman rented additional acreage and leased extra tobacco sheds, but in the postwar years Bradley International Airport swallowed up his farm (and many others) and put him out of business. He died in 1967.

The tobacco-growing population in the middle years of the twentieth century was a polyglot one. In 1982 one retired tobacco buyer said that he had met people along his route from Portland, Connecticut, all the way up to Greenfield, Massachusetts. "They were all nationalities . . . Lithuanians and Polish and Russian and German, and the old Yankees that finally lost their farms—well, sold their farms to the foreign element, because they either didn't have many children or their children didn't want to work it." Yankees remained on some farms, but the Polanders or families of mingled heritage dominated the ranks of small tobacco growers into the late twentieth century, and every member of the family pitched in during the growing and harvesting season. The family children, one of them later recalled, began to work in the fields "as soon as you were big enough to know the plant from the weed." Through those years the fields and sheds of the small and the corporate farms were alive with a cross section of humanity. Men and boys worked in the tobacco while women and girls toiled in the sheds. One small farmer even calculated his juvenile work force at one boy and one girl per acre of leaf in cultivation.

The presence of young people laboring long hot agricultural hours drew the attention of the National Child Labor Committee by the summer of 1917. The Committee was a watchdog group, a major social work organization of the early twentieth century. It aimed "to survey and publicize the facts of child labor," and to see that state laws were enforced. In August Lewis W. Hine, a photographer who worked for the Committee recording child labor conditions across the United States, visited some fifty large or corporate farms along the river, writing a report on "Children and Tobacco in Connecticut," and taking pictures of the laborers. While his view from the fields was not as harsh as his descriptions and images of the industrialized scenes for which he is chiefly remembered, he recorded the same kind of numerical facts, of ages, hours, wages,

and the like about the underage agricultural labor force. "The raising of tobacco has become a highly specialized industry there," he wrote, "employing thousands of workers and comprising the chief output of hundreds of farms, small and large." During the harvest from early August to mid-September the workforce swelled in the "rush to get the leaves ready for curing." The season was short and the supply of itinerant workers limited. "Some are imported from New York and also from nearer cities. Others are transported back and forth daily from Hartford, Springfield and smaller cities. Colored students are brought in from southern colleges and other colored workers are encouraged to settle in the vicinity."

Each morning hundreds of women and children "Polish, Italian, Negro, Lithuanian and Jewish"—were trucked from Hartford for a ten-hour day working tobacco. Although employers said they did not like to hire youngsters, Hine found 1,458 children between the ages of eight and fifteen years on the farms he visited, "and two-thirds of them were from 8 to 13 years old" (see Figure 4). The boys were used as pickers, because they were "more alert [than the men] and can more easily pass between the rows of plants without breaking the leaves" (Figure 11). In the sheds women and girls stood for nine or more hours a day sewing the harvested leaves "on a string which is attached to the flat side of a lath" that was then hung from the frames for drying (Figure 12).

FIGURE 11. Boys "prime" on the Hackell Farm in Buckland, Connecticut, in 1917. Shade-grown tobacco is harvested leaf by leaf, from the ground up, over several days. This requires a small body to crawl between the delicate leaves and a light touch, so children as young as eight years old were often employed. They worked close to the ground, bent into L-shapes, in the high humidity beneath the tents. The photographer's notes give the ages of these boys as thirteen and fourteen. (Photo: Lewis W. Hine for the National Child Labor Committee. Courtesy Photography Collections, University of Maryland, Baltimore County)

FIGURE 12. Hawthorn Farm, Hazardville, Connecticut, 1917. Shade-grown tobacco was hung without the stalks. Women and girls worked inside the sheds manually sewing the leaves onto laths (sewing machines would later speed up the job). The ages of the girls in the foreground are given as eight, nine, and ten. (Photo: Lewis W. Hine for the National Child Labor Committee. Courtesy Photography Collections. University of Maryland, Baltimore County)

Hine's report seems even-handed. He deplored the use of such young people, but he did note that the conditions of work for women and children were for the most part good, that they were well paid, and that the heavy work is done chiefly by adults, "with some notable exceptions such as the cases of young boys dragging heavy baskets and climbing aloft in sheds hanging the leaves on the rafters." And, finally, "a good wholesome atmosphere prevailed everywhere. Many family groups were in evidence, and a most delighted spirit of industry existed." The harvest was over before the school year began. Nonetheless, Hine's final recommendation was for "some definite supervision exercised in order to forestall any possibility of exploitation or over-work. . . . It is not difficult to see that unless some rational stand is taken these matters will gradually become worse as the demand for these workers increases."

Shade-grown tobacco brought with it big companies controlled from cities like Hartford or New York, and the increased production and labor needs brought with them migrant workers. Hine had earlier noted that the demand arose from the scarcity of mature laborers that became more acute with America's entry into World War I. The presence of children in the fields and in the sheds continued to be significant. The war shut off European immigration and led to high-wage jobs in the manufacturing of matériel. New sources of agricultural labor had to be found, so the Connecticut Tobacco Corporation and other large growers began to hire seasonal workers from the black colleges in the South. Some returned home, but many stayed in New England, in adjacent cities and towns if not on the farms. The African American population of Hartford more than doubled between 1910 and 1920.

The same situation arose again during World War II. With tobacco in high demand as an essential crop, and able-bodied men called into military service, the federal government began to import workers from the British West Indies. Just as the Slavic people of mixed nationalities who came during the late nineteenth and early twentieth centuries were lumped together as Polanders, so now the West Indian immigrants were collectively designated "Jamaicans," whether they stemmed from Jamaica, Barbados, the Grenadines, Antigua, or British Honduras. The Jamaican men, English-speaking British subjects, worked under contract with the federal government's War Food Administration. Not all their experiences were positive in this race-conscious country, and some employers exploited the tensions between blacks and whites as a means of controlling the workers, but the "Jamaicans" presented a united front to the farmers and corporations, and they got along better than some migrant blacks. Many had at least a grade school education and found time to pursue other educational programs during their sojourn in the United States. Some of them stayed in this country after the war and established a viable Jamaican presence, especially in Hartford. Unlike the Polanders, the Jamaicans did not move onto the land in great numbers but used their farm labor to establish lives elsewhere. Amos Taylor, who arrived in the Connecticut fields in 1954, brought his family in 1966, and by 1982 had a wife in banking, one daughter in insurance and another in college, and a son in the Air Force. Like many of the Polanders before them, many of the Jamaicans prospered. "The opportunity's here if you want to grasp it," Taylor said. "Whatever I have achieved, it's from the tobacco."

The first arrivals, over 1,300 of them, reached Connecticut from the West Indies in May 1943; their numbers swelled to 2,700 in 1957 and then declined (but there were still an estimated 600 in the fields in 1988, and to this day you will see Jamaicans working tobacco). The first group were quickly sent to the tobacco and potato fields (although some Jamaicans did find work in industry too). They performed all manner of labor on 5,500 acres of shade-grown leaf. George Hudson, trained as a tailor in Jamaica, "used to sew the nets and run the wires" of the tobacco tenting, but other jobs spanned the gamut from camp cook to transplanting, hoeing, and harvesting. Amos Taylor worked as cultivator, cook, and camp manager. Fieldwork was monot-

onous and tiresome, but far from being too strenuous for most of the men. At first the Jamaicans lived in camps or barracks, some better than others, worked long hours in the field, sometimes seven days a week, complained about the cold before the summer heated up, the food before it was adjusted for their diet, and the sanitary facilities, some of which were anything but sanitary. "They worked together, ate together, played together, prayed together, and slept together," according to historian Fay Clarke Johnson. And they proved to be "quick to grasp an operation" and "developed rapidly into good farm hands." Without their help the production of cigar leaf would have suffered, especially during their first years in the fields. Their presence made it possible for the War Food Administration nearly to eliminate the agricultural labor shortage in the area. Like the newly arrived Polanders at the beginning of the century, the Jamaicans helped to keep tobacco production alive during a crisis.

In the 1950s Hispanics from Puerto Rico began to supplant the Jamaicans, and by the 1980s Laotian workers could be found in the fields. From native Americans to recent arrivals, no one group of people can lay claim to the history of tobacco cultivation in the Connecticut River Valley. Small nineteenth- and twentieth-century farms owned by Yankees, Polanders, and Polish Americans, as well as large twentieth-century corporations, like the Hartman Tobacco

Company or the Consolidated Cigar Corporation, which employed a labor force of mixed ethnicity, age, and gender, all participated in the production of this specialized crop (Figure 13).

The history of tobacco in the Valley reflects the history of the United States as an immigrant nation.

FIGURE 13. Putting up cloth, Imperial Agricultural Corporation, DuBon Farm, Windsor, Connecticut. The New England tobacco growers were equal opportunity employers. Both sexes and many migrant and immigrant groups worked on the outdoor and shade-grown farms. Here in 1950s Connecticut a white woman and a black man work side by side hanging cloth onto galvanized wire to form a shade tent. They stand on makeshift sawhorses; some workers walked on stilts while doing this overhead job. (Courtesy Windsor Historical Society)

FIGURE 14. The air curing process is about to begin. This shed is loaded to the doors with freshly harvested tobacco leaves speared on laths hung from beams in three and one-half tiers. The builders mixed two related types of venting in this shed. The vertical vents on the gable end are hinged on the side and swing open like doors. The vents on the flank are hinged on the top and swing out at a slant. There appears to be no venting at the ridge. (Photo: Howes Brothers. Courtesy Ashfield Historical Society)

Tobacco Sheds
Connecticut Valley Vernacular

The wide diversity we find among the tobacco peoples of the Valley is not reflected in the tobacco shed. Its roots in older barn types can be traced, but once the building appeared as a fully realized design, given the consistency through time of its function, it changed almost not at all. It was a highly specialized capital improvement, dedicated to air curing one crop and placed in active use for barely two or three months a year (although for the rest of the time it housed the cured leaves before they were processed for market, was available for equipment and other storage, and sometimes sheltered raccoons and other wild things). There are differences between the sheds raised by small farmers to cure their broadleaf and those built by contractors for the large corporations to hang their shade-grown tobacco, but these are differences in magnitude and detail rather than kind. There are various geometrical arrangements among the members of the frames, and there are at least three variations in the venting patterns, but these are not fundamental distinctions. The original—and pre-sumably anonymous—designers of the tobacco shed got it right from the beginning, and there is no real evolution in its development from the mid-nineteenth to the mid twentieth century. I will therefore emphasize its origin and early development.

In her *Native Genius in Anonymous Architecture*, historian and critic Sibyl Moholy-Nagy pointed out three principal criteria for examining indigenous architecture: "expression of site and climate, expression of form and function, expression of materials and skills." Such buildings, she wrote, exhibit the "unsupplemented use of native building materials and local construction skills," as well as "planning and massing as the result of specific unduplicable functional requirements and site conditions." Vernacular architecture, she added, is "selective, coordinative and coherent." The Connecticut Valley tobacco shed fits the bill exactly.

You usually find the sheds, now, isolated on the intervales at the edge of a field which may contain a variety of crops including corn, potatoes, pumpkins, cucumbers, and tobacco, or perhaps in clusters set side by side, end to end, or scattered (Plate 12). You may also occasionally still see a smaller structure, attached or nearby, that was once used for stripping, sorting, and packing the cured leaves. The small farms probably never had more than a few sheds; those with larger acreage of weed may have had many, now reduced to a few. The plantations of the corporate growers were marked by veritable shed cities. On the small farms sheds were usually erected near the crops for ease of transporting the harvested leaf by horse- or tractor-drawn carts, although some of them stood closer to the house. These buildings are now often put to other purposes, or they are abandoned and intermingled with later structures that effectively obliterate all sense of the original landscape.

It should be recognized at the outset that the tobacco barn is not found exclusively in the Connecticut Valley. Tobacco is raised not only in Maryland, Virginia, Kentucky, Tennessee, and the Carolinas, but in Pennsylvania, Missouri, Wisconsin, New York, parts of Canada, and elsewhere. Heat curing is common in the South, and that process called forth a shed design distinctly different from that of the Valley. Drying sheds in the Pee Dee country of northeastern South Carolina, for example, are roughly twenty feet square in plan and tall in silhouette, with one-story shed roofs flaring out from their sides. An external firebox provides constant heat to the vertical interior where tiers of tobacco hang around a central void. The air drying process in ventilated sheds is also found in many of these venues. Local traditions might indicate differences in sheds from different areas, differences accounted for by the different ways different varieties of tobacco are cured, especially between burley for cigarettes and shade-grown for cigar leaf, but in the main all sheds erected for air curing tobacco are cousins: they are individuals but they are related.

It should also be recognized that when it comes to the details of the design of tobacco sheds in the Connecticut Valley, one builder's rule is another's exception. The instructions for building the sheds found in books and periodicals are not consistent, and the builders themselves tell different tales. There are, however, generalizations to be made. The generic Connecticut Valley tobacco shed is usually a long, relatively low, windowless, horizontal, gabled wooden structure. It is composed of a fixed skeleton and a flexible skin. It is a transverse frame barn, often but not always with gable end openings to allow stalk- or leaf-laden carts and tractors to pass through longitudinally (Plates 13 and 16). Such an arrangement is often called a "drive-through." Two aisles are standard in smaller sheds (see Figure 17 below); three aisles appear in the larger ones commonly erected on the corporate shade plantations. The frames in the small barns are nominally 24 to 30 feet wide and vary in pattern of posts, beams, and diagonal braces (Plates

14–15). Those in larger sheds can reach 32 to 40 or more feet in width. Early on it was common to erect pole barns, with the vertical structural members merely stuck in the ground. Many older barns have poles resting on stone bases. I have seen poles stuck into metal drums set into the soil and filled with concrete. Concrete footings usually mark twentieth-century examples. Floors are universally of dirt unless a shed has been converted to fancier uses.

The frames are usually placed fifteen feet apart along the longitudinal axis and tied to one another by girts. The area defined by the sides of the shed and a pair of frames, containing two bays in a two-aisle design, is called a "bent," and sheds are commonly designated by the number of bents they contain. Thus an "eight-bent shed" will be half the length and hence have half the capacity of a "sixteen-bent shed" of equal width. (A sixteen-bent shed could reach more than 240 feet in length, an uncommon dimension on small farms but not unheard of on larger farms and corporate plantations.) A shed was usually designated by either the number of its bents or its capacity. Around 1900, for example, Irving Allis of Whately, Massachusetts, built an eight-bent shed and later added two more bents, "making the capacity of the barn five acres of harvested tobacco. He had another barn . . . rated for three acres," so by his ratio of field to shed content it must have had six bents. One of these barns was later sold to another grower and moved to East Whately.

Whatever their arrangement of parts, the frames not only hold up the roof and sides of the building, they hold up the drying tobacco as well. Ripe broadleaf is hung by the stalk; shade-grown is hung leaf by leaf. In either case the tobacco is fixed to laths that are placed crosswise to the length of the space and rest on girts along the sides and in the middle of the shed. Those girts not only support the laths of drying tobacco, they also tie the frames together and hold the exterior sheathing. The armature of the tobacco shed is an integrated three-dimensional, skeletal system of support for both the container and its contents.

We have seen that Irving Allis related acreage of harvest to shed size. The relationship between curing shed and agricultural field is a mathematical but not a consistent one. The number and size of sheds a grower will need depends upon the number of acres of leaf he has to cure. Two bents per acre, more or less, is a commonly heard ratio of field to shed. Irving Allis used such a ratio. But one grower recently told me that an acre of leaf fills over three bents in his twenty-four-foot-wide barn, and other growers achieve different results. In his agricultural diary for September 1912 Solomon Terry Wells mentions a four-acre shed. By the ratios just given this could mean roughly either a twelve-bent or an eight-bent barn. The capacity of a shed depends upon its dimensions, the design of its frames, and the method used to hang the tobacco. Methods of hanging can vary from farmer to farmer and, as we have seen, from broadleaf to shade-grown. The number of tiers of laths also varies, from three and a half in small sheds to four and a half in the larger ones. (The "half" is up under the ridge. This extra hanging space is the bonus that results from the ubiquitous gable roof whose primary function, of course, is to shed rainwater.) Classifying sheds by "bents" or "acres," then, may have local meaning but is related to their dimensions and is not a consistent measure in the Valley as a whole.

The acreage of tobacco a farmer planted varied with fluctuations in the market; the amount he harvested depended on his labor, but also upon the weather, pests, blights, and other factors beyond his control. Tobacco could be a lucrative crop, but it was also an uncertain one. The agricultural diary that George Cooley of Amherst, Massachusetts, kept between 1865 and 1885 gives a quick glance at the fluctuations in one farmer's production. As a small grower he could move easily in and out of the market, planting more tobacco in good years and increasing other crops in poor selling seasons. The boom years of the 1860s and 1870s were followed by something of a downturn, and this and other factors affected his income. So did the weather. He mentions tobacco in 1865, but raised not a leaf in 1867. In 1870 he planted 2¾ acres and realized $612.20 for his efforts; the next year he raised 3¾ acres to earn $1267.15. In 1873, 3 acres brought in $741.14, but the following season he

harvested just 2 acres for $195.84. In 1880 he leased his shed to a neighbor, and in the next growing season he shared his acreage with other neighbors. Renting sheds and fields was another common way of adjusting production and curing capacity to a changeful market. The summer of 1882 was dry and he realized only $315. In 1883 he planted 3 acres, of which 2½ were killed by frost. In the next two growing seasons he experienced damage from wind, rain, and hail.

Given the relationship of field crops to shed capacity and the variations of the harvest, sheds had to be easily built and easily altered. The standard design and the ease with which an existing shed could be longitudinally extended by adding bents made it a flexible "machine for curing." But a shed might be enlarged vertically as well as horizontally. In August 1871 Josiah Allen of Deerfield raised his "old tobacco shed" and put in a "new tier" during a time he was expanding his acreage. He must have raised the frames and extended their posts.

The frames are covered with one-inch rough-sawn siding varying in width from, say, 8 to 18 inches, and roofs of (early) shingle or slate, and (later) corrugated sheet metal or asphalt roofing. Eaves usually have generous overhangs to throw rainwater away from the vents below. The shed is designed to remove the water from the leaves by channeling air through itself, but it must also be weather-tight when closed and shed rain in any configuration.

Beneath the roof, the skin of the shed is
flexible; that is, it can easily be closed against
inclement weather or open to the drying breezes.
Three variations in venting patterns create three
different exterior designs. In the most common,
the vertical board exterior, every other or every
third (or more) board forms a vertical vent.
These boards might be hinged on the side and
open like tall narrow doors (Plate 16) or be
hinged at the top to swing out at a slant (Figures
14–15). In the former arrangement the board
turns on metal hinges; in the latter the board may
be hung from similar hinges or on a slat that rests
on a girt. It is then held in place by gravity. The
bottoms of several of these top swinging boards
might be joined by a horizontal cleat so that they
all open with one movement (Plate 17). Hardware ranges from standard off-the-shelf metal
hinges to hooks forged by a local smithy that are
used both to secure the closed vent boards and to
prop them open at a slant. Wide out-swinging
wagon doors in the gable ends can also be
opened for maximum ventilation. They are commonly propped open (or closed) by a piece of
scrap lumber. September in the Valley is characterized by the sight of these barns, with their
open narrow vents swinging or slanting out from
the long sides and gable ends, and the leaves

flashing green and eventually golden-brown from their interior depths.

The advocates of the two methods of vertical ventilation gave contradicting reasons for their preference (and some sheds incorporate both variants). Killebrew and Myrick, for example, admitted that the slanting door will keep sun and rain off the tobacco hanging next to the wall, but they preferred the side-hinged arrangement "as giving the least trouble and better circulation of air." W. W. Garner, on the other hand, advocated top-hinged vents because they furnished protection from direct sunlight and wind while they afforded a larger opening at the bottom, "which is desirable since natural circulation is always upward." While the experts disagreed the farmer-builder was left to his own devices.

The vertical board ventilating systems just described have been associated with the curing of broadleaf tobacco. A second method also has gable-end wagon doors, but uses horizontal siding and thus horizontal openings covered with "blinds" attached to flexible vertical cleats so that several might be opened at once (Figure 16 and Plate 18). It has been noted that this horizontal system of ventilation was commonly used for shade-grown tobacco. There is some truth in this typology, but, as with other aspects of shed design, there would appear to have been no hard and fast rule.

Some growers prefer a third type of ventilation, a variation on the first in which a series of wide wagon doors, one to each bent, open one side of the shed (Plate 19). In this arrangement the shed is loaded from carts entering transversely at the side, rather than driven longitudinally through the building as in the other two venting types. There are no doors on the ends. The ends and the side opposite the doors will usually have vertical vents. It would seem that such sheds serve for curing either broadleaf or shade-grown tobacco. In all these types the roof ventilators vary in shape from a single cupola to monitors running along the ridge to individual metal stacks poking up along the skyline; in some cases there are no roof ventilators. As we have seen, the ultimate design depended upon the individual farmer's understanding of the dynamics of ventilation.

As we might expect, different farmers have different rules about when to open or close the vents. One nineteenth-century reader of the *New England Farmer* gave this account of the method he used in North Hatfield, Massachusetts. When the leaf is newly hung, give it all the air practicable until the initial "sweating" is over. If the weather is hot and sultry, humid or foggy, shut the sheds up tight, but open them as soon as the air dries out. Open the vents for breezes; shut them in rain. After the sweating stage gradually shut the vents more and more to admit less and less air. When the leaves are nearly all cured, open the vents in damp weather and close them in dry weather so that they finish slowly. Shut sheds will

FIGURE 16. A group of field workers at Huntting's Tobacco Farm, Rockwell, Connecticut, 1917. According to the photographer the boys' ages range from nine to fifteen. Although the field in the background is not shaded, the tobacco has been harvested leaf by leaf and is being carried to the sheds in heavily laden, woven wood baskets. The sheds in the right rear are horizontally vented. (Photo: Lewis W. Hine for the National Child Labor Committee. Courtesy Photography Collections, University of Maryland, Baltimore County)

also prevent the wind from blowing the brittle leaves. Once curing is complete, the sheds are shut tight while the leaves wait to be stripped, sorted, boxed, and shipped to the buyer.

The Connecticut Valley shed exists to cure cigar-leaf tobacco, a process that gives the product desirable smoking qualities like texture, color, aroma, and taste. Farmers and agricultural researchers will agree on that, though they disagree on individual design details within the type. Air circulates around the leaves, entering through openings along the sides and exiting through ridge vents. But the character of the ventilation depends on the placement of the shed as well as its openings. There are publications that advise locating the shed in relation to the prevailing breezes, or in an elevated position such as the terrace above the intervale. Some growers say that the east-west orientation of the long axis of the shed is optimal for cross-ventilation; others prefer the opposite direction; and many sheds in the Valley run north and south, and even diagonally to the cardinal points. The structures are most effective when isolated or distanced in the fields, away from trees, for the best air flow, although archival photographs and some existing shed "cities" (such as that near Bradley International Airport in Windsor Locks, Connecticut) show buildings clustered together (Plate 20). There seem to be no fixed rules about placement either, although growers will tell you that some of their sheds cure better than others in different locations or with different orientation.

Especially early in the process, even the air curing system needs occasional heat to maintain proper temperature and humidity control within the shed. In the nineteenth and early twentieth centuries (and on a few farms still today) this was supplied by charcoal fires smoldering in depressions in the dirt floor or iron pots set upon it (Figure 17). Heaters are now usually fueled by propane gas tanks perched outside the sheds. According to a publication of the Connecticut Agricultural Experiment Station at New Haven, firing the sheds not only maintained heat but accelerated leaf wilting and chemical changes during the curing. It also controlled the spread of pole rot, a fungus that attacks the green leaves. It hastened the drying process by accelerating the wilting, thus opening wider spaces between leaves for the passage of air. And it helped produce the desired aroma and taste. But, as with others aspects of the tobacco industry, growers differed in their approach to firing. After discussing the best way to proceed, another expert, L. P. M. Hickey, admitted that "there are almost as many different views on how to fire tobacco in the curing barn as there are farmers." And the *American Agriculturalist* said as early as 1860, "The curing of tobacco . . . is an art that can only be learned by practice." For each farmer, whatever worked became his rule.

Firing often had to be constant for some days, and this required a twenty-four-hour watch by farm laborers. In the darkness the effect could appear enchanting. According to novelist Mildred Savage, "At night . . . [you saw] only the red glow [of the coals] and the shadows, and you smelled the terrifically heavy smell of tobacco, more suffocating in the hot, close air than the sweetest, sickliest incense, and you thought again, as Parrish did now, that it looked like a setting for voodoo." In the application of heat by charcoal fires the tobacco curing process adheres to its primitive origins in the mid-nineteenth century.

The Connecticut Valley tobacco shed was the perfect solution to one agricultural problem—curing the ripe leaves—and once achieved was never significantly, systemically, changed. In the colonial era growers found space to hang the small amounts of tobacco that needed curing for domestic use in parts of existing farm buildings, or, as antiquarian George Sheldon recorded, in one case in Deerfield in 1696, in "ye chamber," or garret of Daniel Belding's house, where his daughter Sarah hid among the leaves during an attack by French Canadian Mohawks. In 1822 the agronomist Samuel Deane wrote of harvested stalks being placed "in the barn or some other building," and hung "in an apartment which is pretty tight." As late as 1866 W. H. White, a grower, although in the midst of describing a "separate building arranged expressly for the purpose" of hanging tobacco, allowed as how "stables and sheds can be used for want of better" facilities. And later still, as many photographs taken in the Valley between 1882 and 1907 by the Howes brothers show, makeshift arrangements for curing in any handy shed continued to be common, especially among small farmers. For the most part, however, after the 1840s Connecticut Valley farmers cured their tobacco in purpose-built sheds.

The frame structure of the tobacco shed is preindustrial. Its long narrow plan, with its interior divided by posts into two or three aisles, also aligns it with an architectural configuration as old as the Middle Ages or older. The Early Christian basilica has a three-aisle nave. The typical range of buildings surrounding the courtyard of a medieval monastery was divided into two or three aisles, whether it was dedicated to the infirmary, refectory, or library. The typical shed looks in plan like a detached wing of a monastic whole. But this is true only in plan. The medieval ranges are vaulted masonry spatial forms, while the tobacco shed is a trabeated structure in wood. And there was certainly no connection between the two in the minds of the shapers of the ventilated hanging house.

That building type was an inherited form adapted to a new function. It seems rather to have evolved from a model closer to hand: the basic and ubiquitous "English barn" brought to southern New England by the earliest colonists. That gabled, story-and-a-half, three-bay timber-framed structure with broad entrances in the middle of its long sides was designed for grain storage. The Connecticut River tobacco cultivators merely adjusted it to the hanging and air drying process their product demanded. At least that is the pedigree suggested by a two-page spread in E. R. Billings's useful *Tobacco* of 1875 (Figure 18). On the verso is a wood engraving of an English barn filled with hanging leaves, captioned "Old Connecticut Tobacco Shed." On the recto is another wood engraving, of a recognizable, fully articulated shed of a type that still dots the Valley landscape. It is a long gabled form with a small house for stripping and sorting the cured leaf to the left, broad double doors on the short side, tall narrow vents extending down its flank, and a roof ventilator. Billings calls it a "Modern Connecticut Tobacco Shed."

Toward the middle of the nineteenth century, as tobacco replaced broom corn as the cash crop of choice among Valley farmers and they began to expand sharply the acreage of broadleaf, the need for a specialized hanging house became obvious. A correspondent writing from Warehouse Point, in what was to become the heart of the tobacco region in Connecticut, told the *Culti-*

OLD CONNECTICUT TOBACCO SHED.

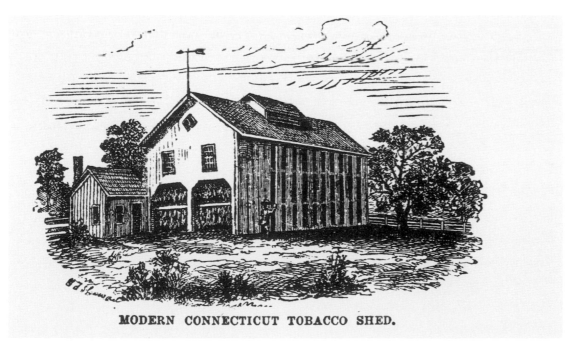

MODERN CONNECTICUT TOBACCO SHED.

FIGURE 18. The purpose-built Connecticut Valley tobacco curing shed appeared during the middle of the nineteenth century. It evolved from the old English barn, a grain storage building that long served for drying the weed. In these wood engravings, which appear on facing pages in E. R. Billings's 1875 *Tobacco*, the English barn is shown as obsolete for curing leaf in the face of the modern tobacco shed. The new model has a stripping shed, vertical side vents, and a ridge vent.

vator in June 1841 that most of the barns used to cure tobacco in his village and vicinity were "built expressly to cure tobacco in." This is the earliest mention I have found of this specialized building type.

As we have seen, tobacco growers in the South often used smoke to cure their leaf. They built tall structures sealed as tightly as possible to contain the smoke during the hanging season. The tobacco fields of Virginia, Kentucky, and South Carolina were marked in late summer by tall, narrow gabled buildings inevitably leaking smoke into the air. Valley tobacco is air cured. The building program this fact implies for a Valley tobacco shed stresses systems of open ventilation and methods of hanging the leaves. Early published discussions of these buildings point to these two factors. Our Warehouse Point commentator noted that in 1841 some two hundred tons of tobacco were grown in his area. He raised two to three acres "as part of my farm-work." The harvested stalks, he went on, should be "carted to the barn and hung upon poles to cure. . . . The barn should be sufficiently ventilated, but not so much open as to expose the tobacco to winds and storms." He recommended a building twenty-four feet wide and as long as wanted. A barn sixty feet long, he said (which would make it a four-bent shed), would usually hold the produce of an acre or one ton on average. (Later, more experienced farmers would develop a more efficient use of space.) He also noted a new

intensity of effort, in that the labor demanded to raise that acre of tobacco was four times that required for an acre of corn.

Another letter to the *Cultivator*, three years later, described the process of growing and harvesting tobacco. Henry Watson of East Windsor, Connecticut, wrote that the cut stalks are "carted to the tobacco sheds for hanging." He went on to detail the method of attaching the leaves to laths with twine (he seems to have detached the leaves rather than spearing the stalks, as would become common with broadleaf) and spacing them about a foot apart, but he said nothing else about these structures, so he must have thought his readers would be familiar with them. These letters suggest that by the end of the 1830s, not surprising in the decade of expanding cigar production in the Valley, the purpose-built tobacco shed had appeared in all its parts. Within a relatively few years the ground was thick with them. The *Gazetteer of Massachusetts* for 1855 counted ninety-seven in the town of Whately alone.

According to the November 1863 issue of the *New England Farmer*, a journal that as we have seen was no friend of tobacco, once the crop was raised and harvested,

the next thing was to *hang* it. . . . The producer turns hangman and looks about for a gallows. The ordinary barns and sheds . . . will not answer. A tobacco shed must be erected. What grows upon an acre and a half will require as much ground as is covered by an average-sized

New England barn. In providing these sheds there must be no delay. . . . All the lumberyards have been stript and every lumber mill . . . has been put to the top of its speed to produce the needful sheds. Every laboring man whom money could induce to work has been detailed to cut, haul and hang it.

He wrote at the beginning of the boom that lasted well beyond the Civil War years, a period of intense building activity.

The earliest datable standing tobacco shed I have come across stems from this period. It was erected at Deerfield between 1852 and 1868 by Elisha Wells and is still in use as an equipment shed on a working farm. Certainly there are others of this age standing in Connecticut and Massachusetts. As did so many of his fellow farmers in this period, Wells abandoned broom corn for tobacco as a commercial crop. He erected an eight-bent, two-aisle shed with sixteen-inch vertical ventilator doors and a continuous louvered ventilator along the ridge of the roof. There is only one sliding wagon door at each end, unlike the common out-swinging, two-door arrangement of longitudinal "drive-throughs." The interior structural and hanging frames are arrangements of hewn and sawn timbers fastened together by pegged mortise and tenon joints that took no account of the Industrial Revolution (see Plate 15). Blackened timbers bear witness to years of charcoal firing.

Wells and other farmers could find information about shed building in their agricultural journals. Brief notices of sheds in the *Cultivator* of the 1840s were followed in other periodicals by descriptions and instructions for building that last through the rest of the century and beyond. In 1857, the Hartford *Homestead* published a pair of articles that began crisply ("put up a good frame; shingle the roof"), bogged down in confusing details of construction, then emphasized the need for "very perfect" ventilation. "Simply a good draft from the ground to the roof is not sufficient, . . . but lateral ventilation is often a great advantage":

The usual plan [the second article continued] is to give the building 24 feet breadth; that is breadth enough to be spanned by two 12 foot rails. The tobacco is hung upon rails in tiers one above the other, about five feet apart, there being three or at most four of these tiers. For the support of the rails strong joists, poles, or planks are put upon the sides of the building, and through the middle of the shed lengthwise; the lower tier of rails being so high that the tobacco will be two feet above the ground, if the shed is not floored.—Ventilation is provided usually at the sides by having the boards forming the side run perpendicularly [that is, vertically], and every other, or third board hung upon hinges to open and shut; a clear circulation being provided under the shed also. A roof ventilation is of great advantage, especially in showery weather, and if the draft secured in this way is good, the lateral ventilators will be only occasionally required. The roof ventilation should extend the entire length of the ridge, and should be provided with valves or blinds to open and shut, and so roofed as to exclude rain entirely. . . . The ventilators should be kept open in all fair weather, except when a strong drying wind blows, in which case it is occasionally best to close those to windward. In rainy weather shut up all tight.

The author also turns his attention to the second prime consideration of the program, the method of hanging the tobacco to dry.

The plants are tied to each side of the rail. . . . Planks are laid for a man to stand upon and bind on the plants. It requires two hands [that is, workers], one to toss or hand up the plants and the other to tie them on [to the "rails," or laths]. . . . Plants that will hang in a five foot space and still give room for a person to work beneath them; that is, which are actually 4½ to 5 feet long may be hung 24 to 28 on a 12 foot rail, (10 to 12 inches apart). Plants that will occupy a four foot space may be hung 30 to 40 on a rail, and the very small plants will go 50 on a rail without damage. The rails should be placed 18 to 20 inches apart.

Mathematical precision permeates all eras and all phases of tobacco culture. Such prescriptions for building sheds were not always followed to the letter of course, but with some changes in terminology and some variations in detail, this describes the bulk of the sheds standing in the Valley today and the method of filling them in August and September.

The 1860s, a decade we remember as one of great prosperity in the New England tobacco fields, saw the publication of any number of such prescriptions for the design of curing sheds. The decade also saw the publication of rudimentary wood-engraved illustrations of these structures. In the *American Agriculturalist* for April 1862 there is a tiny representation of a cross section and perspective view of a small two-aisle shed that is said to be "common in the Connecticut Valley" (Figure 19). It has vertical vents along the side and one roof ventilator. *Tobacco Culture*, which first appeared in 1863, contains similar but more detailed cuts. And by the 1880s barn books such as Robert Shoppell's routinely carried detailed descriptions and illustrations of specific Connecticut Valley tobacco sheds. After 1900 the various publications of state agricultural research stations and the United States Department of Agriculture gave increasingly more precise (albeit varying) instructions for proper shed design and the varying reasons for their recommendations. Farmers remained free to follow these or not.

The number of discussions of tobacco culture published in agricultural journals from the 1850s and '60s on suggests the growing interest in this cash crop. The repeated descriptions and illustrations of tobacco sheds point to the fact that the farmers themselves were usually the builders of these essential capital improvements. As Billings wrote in *Tobacco*, the grower's chief expenses in raising this crop were the cost of fer-

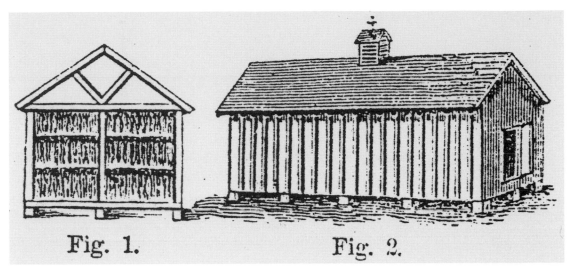

FIGURE 19. This rudimentary wood engraving of a two-aisle tobacco shed appeared in "Hints on Tobacco Culture, No. II," in *American Agriculturalist*, April 1862. It is one of the earliest published illustrations of the new Connecticut Valley building type. "The building is framed 24 feet wide, the posts 16 feet high. . . . In fastening on the outside boarding, about every third board is hung on hinges, making openings from top to bottom. Ventilators are placed in the shingled roof. . . . These 'sheds' are set up some 18 inches from the ground. . . . They have no floors, and are of indefinite length." This early barn has a raised floor that would be rare in later sheds, and a truss area not used for hanging as it would be soon.

tilizer, labor, and sheds (the enormous cost of tenting the intervales came later). The land must be enriched, the growing plants tended by field hands, and the tobacco cured before it is sent to market. As one optimistic farmer recently said, "Growing tobacco is not a problem, you have to have a barn to hang it in."

Small farmers could not afford to hire builders to erect their barns. Nineteenth-century agricultural diaries demonstrate that construction of and repairs to farm structures were constant and time-consuming parts of farm work. The diary of Julius Robbins of West Deerfield, which

begins in 1840 and first mentions tobacco in 1862, records his joining in at frequent barn and shed "raisings" by his neighbors. Solomon Terry Wells of East Windsor, Connecticut, who was then seventy-five years old, mentions helping two different neighbors "raise a tobacco shed" during May and again in June 1906. With a gang of friends helping, a shed would go up relatively quickly, depending of course on its size. The diary of Alden Briggs records that, with the daily (except the Sabbath) assistance of one or two hired hands, he put up his "new" tobacco shed between the August 1, 1892, when they "drew logs" from the mill and dug holes for the poles (which were "set" on the third), and the August 25, when the roof was shingled and the building complete. Cutting tobacco then commenced, and by the first of September the "new barn" was filled.

Briggs's shed, as far as we know from his notes, went up without a problem, but that was not always the case among amateur builders. Exactly one year after he finished his work in South Deerfield, the Blodgett family, living on Terry (now King's) Island in the river north of Windsor Locks, Connecticut, began its own shed. In his diary for 1893, seventeen-year-old George Blodgett recorded that they "cut the posts for the shead" on August second, "drawed" posts on the third, "squared the shead and dug 7 holes [and] drawed sum more poles" on the fourth. The next day they sunk more postholes and prepared the "plates" in anticipation of the sixth when they "Raised the tobacco shead." This seems to mean that in five days they had acquired the main structural members, laid out the plan of the shed on the ground, dug the holes for the vertical supports, lifted them into place, and tied them together with horizontal members. Work of covering the frames went forward steadily (as did work in the fields) until the roof boards were nearly all in place (they used factory-produced wire spikes and nails). Then disaster struck. On August 29 a hard southeast storm brought winds that "hurt" the tobacco in the fields and "Broke

the trease down." The next day was worse: "the Tobacco shead Blew down All to Smash," wrote George, adding that they dismantled what was left standing and "piled up the stuf." On August 31 they began all over again. Since the lumber was measured and cut (and they probably worked long hours to get ready for the fast-approaching harvest of the undamaged crop), rebuilding went quickly, and the shed was presumably filled by September 17, when they "finished cutting Tobacco." High winds are a constant threat to tobacco sheds.

There is a great deal of conflicting testimony about how to build sheds and how sheds were built. Again, some generalizations are in order. Typically of hewn or sawn chestnut (later hemlock and pine) full-dimension timbers, the frames were usually fastened together with mortise, tenon, and pegs in the nineteenth century and more likely with spikes and iron straps in the twentieth. Despite the use of power saws and manufactured nails, these frames carry the era of preindustrial technology far beyond the rise of the Industrial Revolution. In the years that concern us here, the pace of agriculture in the Valley moved more slowly than the pace of industry. Varieties of wood were used in the sheds for different purposes, according to a local grower-builder who has been farming and framing since the middle of the twentieth century. He used old chestnut, which had "the workability of pine and the strength of oak," or hemlock when chestnut was no longer readily available after the mid-twentieth century, for structural members. He also used hemlock for roof sheathing because it "held nails better than pine," which was used for siding and doors because "it holds together better." This is one man's wisdom. Another builder, who has also dismantled many sheds, agreed that hemlock was common for structure and white pine for siding, but he also pointed out that sheds might be built of any wood at hand in the farmer's wood lot. He once pulled down a shed built entirely of maple. Every nail in it was bent.

There have been some attempts to create a catalogue of frame types. A study of 102 surviving sheds in Deerfield, Massachusetts, diagramed three methods of bracing interior frames for two-aisle structures: a group in which the diagonals coming off the top of the central post stop at the uppermost transverse rail to form a "Y"; a group in which they form a "V" by continuing to the underside of the gable; and a group in which the diagonals begin midway up the side and central posts and meet above each of the aisles to form an "M," or, more accurately, an inverted "W" (Figure 20). The latter arrangement is quite common. Such scholarly investigations have their place and these configurations certainly exist, but there are other variations and many alterations as well. And a good blow that rocks a shed will generally call forth additional bracing that often spoils the neatness of the original figure.

Whatever the pattern of the framing members, according to Killebrew and Myrick they ought to be timbers of good size, and not just on account of the great weight of the freshly harvested leaves. They recommended 7 x 7 posts, plates, and beams, 6 x 6 main girts, and 4 x 6 outside girts. It is better to "build a substantial structure at a somewhat increased cost, than to erect a frail structure that the first big wind might blow down." Despite such warnings, small farmers often built hastily and cheaply, creating relatively light, flimsy structures that, with vents closed, offered broad flanks to the onrushing gale. A good blow might shake a shed, or it might knock it over. Charles Hoffmann, who farmed in New Preston, in the Housatonic Valley west of the Connecticut, recorded in late February 1886 that his "Fathers Tobacco Barn had blown down . . . & his Ice house ruf blowd of[f]." The same wind took a neighbor's shed, too.

The hurricane of 1938 was the mother of all such storms. Sunderland, Massachusetts, alone lost forty sheds in that blow. Enoch Pelton later remembered that most of the tobacco had been harvested when the winds hit Connecticut that September. They "took the barns and the tobacco, . . . the whole works. . . . I dare say a third of the sheds went down in this valley." Chester Woodford of Avon, Connecticut, remembered that "We were firing the shed . . . with . . . charcoal, and had a fireman in there watching the stoves and all of a sudden the darn shed blew down because there was a hurricane." (The fireman was miracu-

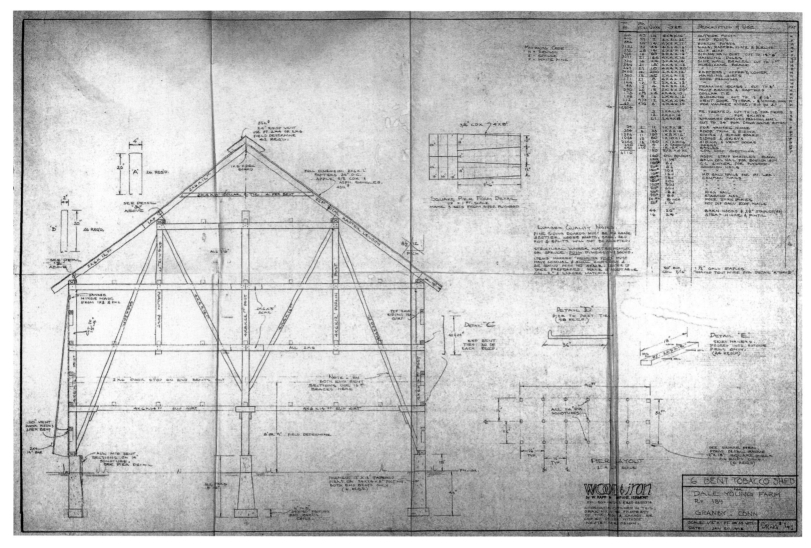

FIGURE 20. Vernacular architecture may be of the earth, but it does not grow spontaneously like a mushroom. This is a one-sheet contract document for a six-bent shed erected in Granby, Connecticut, in 1998. It shows a two-aisle plan with frames braced in an inverted "W" pattern, and out-swinging vent boards. This design draws on more than a century of experience in shed building and demonstrates that a few sheds are still rising despite the general downturn in tobacco production. (Courtesy Walter K. Rapp)

lously unhurt.) Such setbacks merely brought out the resiliency of tobacco growers. "The day after the hurricane my sister and I went out . . . to look at the damage," one Windsor, Connecticut, woman recalled. "The sheds were just flat . . . [and] we were walking around on the broken pieces. . . . My father was already making plans . . . to rebuild . . . and start all over." Emil Mulnite also lost his sheds, but he had replaced one with re-used lumber by November, had a second up by December, and had five in service by the next September, when he harvested 25 acres of tobacco. As Chester Woodford put it, people stayed in tobacco despite the hazards because they "dream[t] of a killing once in a while."

According to Solomon Wells's diary, within two weeks in September 1912 "Wm. Thompson had a 4 acre tobacco shed full of tobacco blown down," and "H. W. Talcott's tobacco shed full of tobacco was burned." Another hazard is fire. A shed, whether or not it is full of cured tobacco, is a tinderbox. Abandoned sheds are tempting targets for arson. The blaze depicted as a climactic event in the movie version of Mildred Savage's *Parrish* (1961) was not just a plot device. "Dennis Bryon's house, barn & tobacco shed were burned last night," Solomon Wells reported to his diary in mid-December 1898. "A tobacco shed burned down. That's just one of the hazards of the business," a retired Windsor grower told an interviewer in 1995. Almost any tobacco farmer in the Valley who has reached senior status, can tell

tales of fire, collapse, and other disasters. But the tobacco shed also proved to be resilient, a flexible, simple structure, easily erected, easily repaired, easily altered, easily wracked, and easily replaced. It exemplifies the buoyancy of the farmers who filled it.

It could also be easily moved. Wind is not the only force to take down sheds. "They were made to be portable," in the words of one local observer. Moving sheds, barns, or houses was a common occurrence recorded in nineteenth-century agricultural diaries. Farm structures could be moved whole, on skids, or, when frames were assembled on the ground and raised into place one by one then covered with siding and roofing, they were easily dismantled. It is a mark of the flexibility of these structures that they can come down by the reverse of the process by which they were built, and they can be moved in parts from one site to another. We have seen that one of Irving Allis's Whately sheds was moved in the early twentieth century. Another farmer in Suffield, Connecticut, in the course of reducing the size of his tobacco crop, recently dismantled a distant seven-bent shed, moved it on a flatbed truck, and re-erected it on a new site nearer his house.

Home-grown craftsmanship is still characteristic of some shed building. All over the area during the recent boomlet in cigar smoking and hence high tobacco prices, while some abandoned sheds were melting into the ground, others were being refurbished by the growers themselves as they planted to meet the demand, at least one of them using lumber cut and sawn on his own property. In the twentieth century, however, neighborhood shed raisings were paralleled by the appearance of the professional builder who erected smaller sheds for farmers and larger ones for corporate growers. For example, in the Luddy/Taylor Connecticut Valley Tobacco Museum there is a receipt for $163.50 recording payment by Henry Scott of Windsor to Emil Weber "For building tobacco shed . . . 64 ft long" in August 1918. The terse mention of the longitudinal dimension was all that was needed since builder and grower both knew that would translate into a four-bent shed. A builder out of Glastonbury, Connecticut, named Ernest Mackay hired a crew of twenty-eight to travel the Valley to erect sheds in the 1920s and 1930s. They would put up a substantial shed in a week. Frank Betsold and his sons built any number of houses and sheds in Hatfield during the middle of the century.

As late as the 1980s and 1990s Walter "Skip" Rapp put up sheds for corporate and other large growers in Connecticut (Figures 20, 21). He kept a basic six-man crew, and with a crew of nine could put up a sixteen-bent, 320-foot-long corporate shed in about two months. In 1997, for example, he designed and erected a sixteen-bent shed for Frank Zera, Jr. in Suffield, a building 32 feet wide and enclosing 8,100 square feet, at a cost of about $90,000. In the late 1990s Rapp moved old sheds and built new ones for a plantation near Bradley International Airport. Such an investment stood in sharp contrast to scenes elsewhere in the Valley, where older sheds were slowly vanishing from the landscape.

Zera's shed is unusual for its late date but not for its size. The area north of Hartford remains the heart of what is left of the shade-grown industry, as it has been for the last century. Shade-grown is corporate-grown, or at least corporate-controlled, and the corporations tend to build large sheds. The nominally 24-foot wide, two-aisle drive-through structure with two doors in the gable end of the smaller farmer is replaced by sheds wider by some eight feet or more with three aisles. The corporations deal in large quantities of leaf, and a shed's capacity for curing tobacco is greatly increased by these enlarged features, yet sheds of this size did not appear only with the era of shade grown leaf. An article on tobacco cultivation by J. M. Crafts published in *Country Gentleman* in March 1864 described "the best form of shed" as one that was 38 to 40 feet wide having three aisles. Still, W. W. Gardner noted in 1909 that, while increased size meant economy, and "the best barn was the cheapest," larger barns increased the difficulty of proper ventilation. And he reiterated that two principles should govern shed design: it should be as airtight as possible and provide for an efficient system of ventilation. The smaller shed remains more common than the larger one.

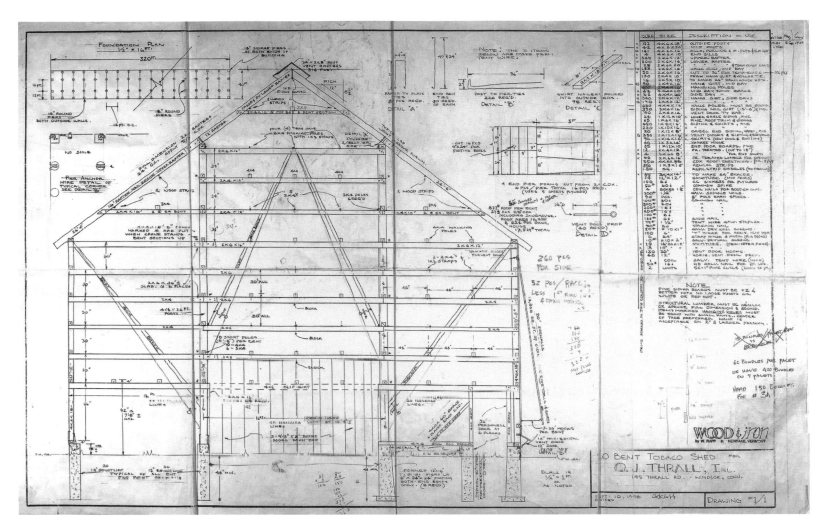

FIGURE 21. The Connecticut Valley tobacco shed was a designed artifact, whether it was cobbled together by a farmer-builder in the mid-nineteenth century or erected from a working drawing in the late twentieth. This is a 1998 design for a large corporate tobacco shed. Forty feet wide, it contains 12,800 square feet, and its 16 bents stretch 320 feet on the long axis. The diagrammatic plan locates the concrete piers; the section shows a three-aisle frame with diagonal bracing and out-swinging vent boards. Such a recent capital investment attests to the fact that cigar-leaf tobacco is still grown under shade in the Valley, although the acreage under cultivation is vastly diminished from the glory days of the 1920s. (Courtesy Walter K. Rapp)

Gardner prescribed a shed 32 feet wide with frames at 16-foot spacing, and recommended no more than three tiers of hanging tobacco. Posts, plates, and beams used for the frame should be substantial, at least 7 by 7 inches, he said, for each bent of his recommended dimensions could hold 4,500 plants, which when green would weigh at least ten tons. There should also be a horizontal ventilator for admitting air below the sills. He recognized both vertical and horizontal side venting systems, but he did not recommend the arrangement of ventilation by vertical side doors because he thought such a shed was harder to weatherproof. Instructions of this kind set a twentieth-century standard for shed construction that was more or less followed, more or less ignored, by the farmers and builders who actually placed the sheds on the intervales.

The curing shed may be the most conspicuous architectural type associated with the tobacco fields, but it is not the only distinctive seasonal building found in the vicinity of the crops, especially the crops of family farms. The tobacco cured in the hanging house during late summer and autumn then awaited the next step in the process, the stripping and sorting that went on in winter. The area devoted to preparing the leaf for market needed two characteristics: it should be warm and humid. Josiah Allen of Deerfield, who had no stripping shed in 1867, reported to his diary in November of that year that he and a hired hand were stripping tobacco in the "back room" (presumably of his house) because it was "too cold & dry [to] strip in shed." By 1870 he had set up a stove in the shed but nonetheless found it necessary to move into the "back kitchen" to work. By 1871 he had fitted out a proper stripping room. There heat and humidity produced the atmosphere essential to working with the delicate plants.

"A chimney rises . . . through the roof, enabling us to put in a stove . . . in which we may have a fire to strip by in cold weather," according to W. H. White's 1874 account of his own stripping room in the *American Farmer*. The curing shed housed tobacco through fall and early winter; in winter people worked and socialized in the stripping shed. Once the tobacco cured it had to be stripped (in the case of broadleaf that had been hung on its stalk) and sorted ("assorted," according to Josiah Allen of Deerfield) into leaves suitable for wrapper, binder, or filler. This preparation of the leaf for the buyer might occur any time from late October through the rest of the winter, and it was usually carried on in a special room that was part of, attached to, or in the vicinity of the tobacco shed. It may be recognized by its lower gable roof, its chimney, or its rows of basement windows (Plates 21, 22; Figure 22). The latter feature reflects the presence of a

FIGURE 22. A house-proud mother and son stand before a domestic establishment paid for, at least in part, by good times in the nineteenth-century tobacco market. To the left rear of the house is a large tobacco shed with ridge ventilator in the form of a rare ornamental cupola, a chimney at the gable end, and basement windows. The last two features signal the presence of a stripping room beneath this end of the shed. Broadleaf was hung on the stalk to cure, and had to be stripped from the stalk before grading and shipping to a buyer. This was winter work, and a stove warming the room was welcome. Handling the delicate leaves was best done in the humid atmosphere of a cellar lit by windows at grade level. (Photo: Howes Brothers. Courtesy Ashfield Historical Society)

FIGURE 23. Men, women, and a boy sort leaves preparatory to shipping to a buyer about 1900. Skylights and oil lamps supply the illumination. This is the last stop for the leaf before it leaves the farm. During such periods of indoor communal labor mouths were as busy as hands. Family lore passed into oral history among farmers and their help as well as from generation to generation in the stripping and sorting rooms of the tobacco farms. (Photo: Howes Brothers. Courtesy Ashfield Historical Society)

"tobacco cellar," a half-sunken, well-lighted area with a dirt floor. Its humidity softened the brittle leaves and made them easier to handle. This feature appeared early; it is mentioned in the *American Agriculturalist* in 1863. In another letter, in this case to the *Cultivator and Country Gentleman* of February 1866, the prolix Mr. White noted that a "basement room under a part or all of the . . . [curing barn], is convenient for stripping, packing, etc."

On the tobacco farm the lighter indoor chores were largely distaff work, although the agricultural diaries demonstrate that men and boys did the stripping, with women and girls occasionally chipping in when necessary. Hands and mouths worked in unison, often far into the night, by lantern light since few sheds to this day are electrified. According to the 1967 reminiscences of one senior farm worker in Glastonbury, Connecticut, the tobacco cellar was not only a place of toil but the scene of storytelling as well. "While they worked at the tedious sorting, they talked," he said (Figure 23). The oldsters recalled bygone events for the youngsters who worked beside them, thus continuing well into the twentieth century an oral tradition of local history.

FIGURE 24. A classic Connecticut Valley tobacco curing shed about 1900. In this case the vertical vents are joined by lateral wagon doors. The change of value of the roof shingles and siding boards at the far end suggests a recent longitudinal addition of a bent or two. Shed capacity could be easily adjusted to increased crop acreage due to expanding markets. (Photo: Howes Brothers. Courtesy Ashfield Historical Society)

"How Beautiful Is Use"

The Connecticut Valley tobacco shed is a vernacular building type peculiar to a place and time (Figure 24). A necessary byproduct of one episode in the agricultural history of the region, an episode that is slowly coming to an end, the shed lingers into the present in greatly reduced numbers. A "machine for curing," it represents native genius in harnessing the breezes to serve the farmer. It is a historical relic with a doubtful future. But is it architecture? It has certainly been largely overlooked in writings about the Valley in favor of the more familiar, more comfortable, domestic vernacular found at Historic Deerfield and other Valley locations. The public has traditionally favored the romantic over the utilitarian past, and some critics have excluded utility as a basis of architecture.

I think the Connecticut Valley tobacco shed and the shade tent are worthy of our attention as relics of a passing phase of agricultural history, *and* as works of architecture with an aesthetic dimension. It is true that the simple, unsubstantial shed exists solely to answer one utilitarian purpose. So appropriately shaped for seasonally repetitive service, the type never evolved. As vernacular architecture set close to function, it need not change its looks, like an automobile or a dress, with every passing shift of fashion. It sports not even the minimal ornament found on farm buildings in other agricultural areas. How can such an unpretentious, undecorated, flimsy utilitarian building, unintended for human habitation or ritual, be considered architecture?

Whether it is architecture or not depends on one's definition. There is certainly a long list of distinguished observers who would not think of the Connecticut Valley tobacco shed as architecture. According to the influential nineteenth-century critic John Ruskin: "Architecture concerns itself only with those characters of an edifice which are above and beyond its common use," he writes in *The Seven Lamps of Architecture* (1849). A "bicycle shed is a building; Lincoln Cathedral is a piece of architecture" begins historian Nikolaus Pevsner's *Outline of European Architecture* (1943). These worthies, one English, the other Anglo-Teutonic, saw a clear distinction between mere building and sublime architecture, between utility and beauty. They tipped the critical scales towards the art in architecture. Theirs was an elitist and Anglo-Continental stance. But theirs was just one definition of architecture.

At the present time there are signature architects in the United States who cleave to the elite views of Ruskin and Pevsner, who neglect utility as a generator of ideal form. In nineteenth-century America, on the other hand, there were architects, critics, and philosophers who emphasized utility above other considerations; for them it is the starting point in defining architecture. But we must be precise about our definition of utility, too. The various meanings of "function" should be recognized. The famous American architect Louis Sullivan, for example, applied his adage that "form ever follows function" metaphorically. He meant that patterns of building and its ornament (especially its ornament, a Ruskinian consideration) should be inspired by patterns of growth in nature. Architectural historians celebrate his metaphorical use of "function." In the present context its meaning is actual, and that actuality accounts for the special beauty found in vernacular forms.

Vernacular building originates in use. The Connecticut Valley tobacco shed evolved in answer to specific requirements of structure and function: the interior frames form an armature upholding both the board envelope and the dry-ing leaves, and the long silhouette with ventilated gable roof and long straight ventilated sides is the visible expression of the air curing process. The sheds harness the breezes to provide a service to people, just as do windmills or sailboats. And therein lies their beauty. With sculptor and critic Horatio Greenough, who, in writings coeval with the origin of the Valley tobacco shed saw architectural lessons in mechanical function, others, too, have found beauty in the fitness of a form as the direct expression of purpose. Greenough echoed the ideas of the nineteenth-century New England transcendentalists, men like Henry Fowle Durant, whose adage "all beauty is the flower of use" I quoted earlier, Ralph Waldo Emerson, or Emerson's friend, the Rev. William Henry Furness (father of the celebrated Philadelphia architect Frank Furness). The Rev. Furness's aesthetic creed is contained in his succinct exclamation, "how beautiful is use! Fitness is beauty." Even celebrated twentieth-century high-style Boston architect Ralph Adams Cram translated that into a characterization of the English cottage, which, he wrote, "possesses in the highest degree perfect adaptation to function, and therefore absolute beauty." The esthetic jolt I experienced when I first seriously encountered the Valley tobacco barn originated in this critical tradition. I recognized in the shed a fundamental principle of good building: that its forms evolve directly from the purpose for which it was created. A building that does that needs no ornament to generate beauty in the eye of the thoughtful beholder.

Beauty *is*, of course, in the eye of the beholder. It is subjective. Nor need it be intentional. Certainly the first shed builders had no aesthetic aims. Ranks of sheds lining a tobacco field might appear to those with an eye for the picturesque "as though they had been grouped by the hand of taste rather than by that of industry," as one nineteenth-century traveler wrote of similar buildings clustered along the Hudson River, but they are not. The tobacco shed was not created to evoke a sensory response. And yet it does. Empty, with daylight filtering through cracks between siding boards and glancing off airborne motes, or full, with tiers of great browning and aromatic leaves occupying most of the space, these long, twilit tunnels have their own sensuous appeal. Children and migrants who labored in the fields and sheds probably did not pause to admire the lines of these buildings, and workmen sweating in those hot dusty interiors at hanging time may not stop to notice the character of their surroundings—or the environmental hazards therein—but talk to a farmer-builder in a rare moment of leisure (after a day's labor erecting or repairing a shed, or after the weed is safely housed), and he is likely to express in his own vernacular speech an appreciation for these structures that is akin to aesthetic. It is the total ambience that tells. As the daughter of one grower remembered: "I used to love to go with my father in the fall when the tobacco was curing in the sheds at night. . . . I loved the smell of tobacco curing. . . . And it was fun to help dad close the sheds or open them a little more." The novelist Mary Ellen Chase, a resident of the Valley, also saw beauty in the sheds scattered about the local landscape: "One never looks upon them without wondering with gratitude at the wisdom shown in their length and contour, at the way in which they suit the wide fields where they stand with the hot sun penetrating the long, perpendicular openings in their sides and glowing upon their wooden clapboards." The painting by W. N. Wilson on the dust jacket of her book is a view of the Valley in which hanging houses settle compatibly onto the intervale. The sheds, to borrow from Emerson, "nestle in nature," and draw "meaning from her roots and grains."

The beauty of the tobacco shed does not derive from decorative refinements. There are no Greek Revival returns, no Pennsylvania Dutch hexes, no hammered metal weather vanes to be found on these vernacular buildings. Economics joins function in shaping them. And while the beauty of the shed derives initially from the fitness of shape to need, site, and cost, over time it is enhanced by its melding with the agricultural environment. The appeal of the shed stems not only from purposive form but from what nineteenth-century English designer William Morris called "the rust of time" as well. By this he meant that the effects of age—the result of use over time—enhance original beauty (Plate 21). Marks of the flow of the seasons show in the groups of weatherbeaten sheds toeing the riverbanks, defining the fields, or silhouetted against river and hills. These marks include the smoke-stained interior frames and boards, many of which bear the scars of axe or adze; warped and sun-baked exteriors of sere untreated wood or faded and peeling paint; corroded hardware, patchwork repairs to walls and roofs; cracked slate or collapsing sheet-iron; sagging eaves and ridges. Sheds that are actively used reflect the annual cycle of the seasons. The many that are abandoned record a longer passage. They are the three-dimensional timelines of regional history.

Whether built by skilled farmer or professional framer, these are designed artifacts. As Thomas Schlereth, a student of material culture, has written, "the existence of a man-made object is concrete evidence of [the] presence of a human mind operating at the time of fabrication." In full function, with vents open to the late summer breezes, these seasoned structures are richly sculpted by mellow sunlight and moving shadows. This is architecture created without ego, without an eye to the shifts of stylistic fashion, but it is architecture nonetheless: the environmentally sensitive and visually satisfying result of conscious decisions about need, cost, and available materials and talents. The tobacco shed is the perfect manifestation of Sibyl Moholy-Nagy's expressions of "site and climate," "form and function," and "materials and skills." It is a true example of what Frank Lloyd Wright called "beautiful and often instructive" because "intimately related to environment and to the heart-life of the people."

The Waning of the Sheds

The Connecticut River tobacco curing shed had its origin in the early nineteenth century. Survivors constitute one of the Valley's most ubiquitous traditional architectural types. The landscape of the lower Valley is characterized by their presence as well as the diminished but lingering existence of the textile covered frames of the shaded fields. The history of the many immigrant peoples who have worked on the intervales beneath the hot sun or in the humidity beneath the cloth is recalled by these flimsy monuments. With each shed that collapses from neglect, goes up in flame, or is removed to save taxes, to resell its timbers, or to be replaced by another building, with each historically shaded acre that remains unplanted, the Valley loses one more piece of its special character.

The agricultural landscape survives in some

FIGURE 25. A moldering shed off River Road in Hatfield, Massachusetts, 2000. The Valley is dotted with abandoned and decaying sheds like this one. With the slow demise of the cultivation of cigar-leaf tobacco, especially among small farmers, most examples of the region's characteristic vernacular architecture will vanish within a generation. (Photo: author)

areas, but it is slowing vanishing. Across the region commercial and residential development is replacing fields of crops. Suburban sprawl gobbles up land, bringing with it *arrivistes* who object to the proximity of agricultural odors, migrant laborers, and chemical sprays. In sections such as that between Bradley International Airport and Hartford on the west side of the river—the heart of the old shade-growing district—high-tech industries packed into shiny metal and glass boxes, commercial strips, and suburban chipboard housing estates are crowding out the waning tobacco fields, making an architectural no-man's land out of what was once a distinctive vernacular landscape (Plate 24). "Yes, it's growing buildings now where I grew tobacco, shopping centers and schools and industrial buildings, office buildings," said one retired farmer recently. With the changes in the market after World War II, the development of homogenized wrappers (made by machines from scrap rather than whole leaves), and growing evidence of the hazards of smoking even cigars, many small farmers gave up the crop, and many of the tobacco companies stopped buying from their contract growers, began to liquidate their vast land holdings, and went out of business. So, for example, after the Hartman Tobacco Company ceased production following the 1978 season, one of its plantations became the Buckland Mall.

However flimsy they are, the tobacco sheds are man-made extensions of the agricultural landscape, lovely examples of vernacular architecture, and mementos of the peoples who have worked the Valley. But with the inevitable demise of the tobacco industry they will become obsolete, and, since they were specifically designed and economically built for one purpose only, they are not easily upgraded to other uses (Plate 25). The Luddy/Taylor Connecticut Valley Tobacco Museum in Windsor is dedicated to remembering this episode of Valley life, and it displays photographs and tools of the industry as well as a large three-aisle shed that will presumably survive. The Hatfield Historical Commission in Massachusetts has seen to the restoration of the Billings Way tobacco barn as an historic landmark and farm museum. It is 30 feet wide, eight bents long, with frames of pegged mortise-and-tenon joinery. But these "decommissioned" sheds are compromised and scrubbed up versions of their former selves. They have concrete floors, tight boarding, electricity, plans for plumbing, and only a token display of tobacco hanging on laths. They have lost William Morris's rust of time. I am happy to have them, and, at the same time, a little saddened by their fate. They represent trophy preservation. It is the hundreds of unrestored sheds dotting the Valley in Connecticut and Massachusetts that are the crucial features of the local scene.

Only if many, many sheds are stabilized and not overly restored will the Valley landscape retain its special character. But this is not in the cards. Change happens. Loss is inevitable. Buildings like people have finite life. Mere mortals can only stand aside as this fragile and beautiful architecture meets "its death at the hands of the slow perpetual decay of nature." We are witnessing the waning of a remarkable vernacular environment (Figure 25; Plate 26).

NOTES

INTRODUCTION

P. 3: *"a calendar based"*: Simeti, *On Persephone's Island*, 78.

P. 3: *"to crack them open"*: Glassie, *Vernacular Architecture*, 21.

P. 4. *"All beauty is the flower of use"*: Henry Fowle Durant, "The Spirit of the College," unpublished talk, 1877 (Wellesley College Archives).

P. 4: *"Utilitas, Firmitas, Venustas"*: Vitruvius, *Ten Books on Architecture*, 17.

P. 4: *A glance at a topographical map*: see Jorgensen, *Guide to New England's Landscape*, 19.

P. 5: *"the simplification of language"*: Baird, *The Most of It*, 223.

P. 6: *"hanging house"*: Billings, *Tobacco*, 315.

P. 8: *not the only building types*: Another type of structure associated with tobacco (and other) farms is the barracks housing migrant or immigrant laborers. These standard forms belong more to the sociology of labor then to the history of architecture.

P. 8: *"folk-structures"*: Wright, "The Sovereignty of the Individual," 85.

TOBACCO FIELDS

P. 11: *"Sweet and winsome"*: Bacon, *The Connecticut River*, 346. Various sources on the Valley give varying statistics; mine are nominal.

P. 11: *"often a series"*: Jorgensen, *Guide to New England's Landscape*, 48–59.

P. 12: *"great areas of meadow"*. Ferber, *American Beauty*, 33.

P. 12: *"spacious and fertile meadow"*: Samuel Peters, *A General History of Connecticut* (1782), in Bell, *Face of Connecticut*, 1985.

P. 12: *"Their universal fertility"*: Dwight, *Travels in New England*, 2: 226–29; see also 1: 218.

P. 12: *"the imagination can scarcely conceive"*: Thomas Cole, "Essay on American Scenery" (1836), in McCoubrey, *American Art*, 106.

P. 12: *"Long strings of farmsteads"*: Wood, *New Eng-*

land Village, 22, 34–35. See also Thomson, *Changing Face of New England*, 41.

P. 14: *long oval shape*: compare the map in Jorgenson, *Guide to New England Landscape*, 127, to that in Bell, *Face of Connecticut*, 27.

P. 14: *"hold the moisture"*: Bain and Meyerhoff, *Flow of Time*, 7.

P. 14: *"crazes"*: Garrison, *Landscape and Material Culture*, 65–93.

P. 15: *"in fertile and well-dunged ground"*: Cabrera Infante, *Holy Smoke*, 10.

P. 15: *"mile on mile"*: Ferber, *American Beauty*, 186.

P. 15: *"who would have thought"*: "Tobacco in Hampshire County."

TOBACCO LEAVES

P. 17: *Long Nines*: see Heimann, *Tobacco and Americans*, 80–111.

P. 17: *"has been very largely entered into"*: *Report of the [U.S.] Commissioner of Patents*, 1845, 264.

P. 17: Whately statistics: Temple, *History of the Town of Whately*, 175–77.

P. 17: Suffield statistic: Alcorn, *Biography of a Town: Suffield*, 141.

P. 17: *"The best tobacco for wrappers"*: *Daily Picayune*, 16 September 1863.

P. 17: Horace Wolcott Account Book: Connecticut Historical Society.

P. 18: Henry Watson: "Tobacco in Connecticut."

P. 18 *From seedbed to curing shed*: see, for examples, Charles Hoffmann Record Book (Connecticut Historical Society), Josiah Allen Journals (Pocumtuck Valley Memorial Association), and Robinson, *Facts for Farmers*, 960–62.

P. 18: *"Tobacco like a baby"*: Savage, *Parrish*, 35.

P. 18: *"Tobacco was for the"*: Cane, *Whately*, 74.

P. 18: *"Thunder showers with hail"*: Solomon Terry Wells Diaries, 28 August 1912 (Connecticut Historical Society).

P. 18: *"That even cut off some of the stalks"*: Emil Mulnite, oral history statement, 1982 (Thomas J. Dodd Research Center).

P. 18: *"Oh yes, I've been 'through the mill'"*: Stanley Waldron, oral history statement, 1995 (Luddy/Taylor Tobacco History Museum).

P. 18: *"Gee, we had a lot of tobacco"*: Chester Woodford, oral history statement, 1982 (Thomas J. Dodd Research Center).

P. 19: *"disagreeable and hard"*: "Tobacco Versus Useful Crops."

P. 19: *"Hot as mustard"*: James Bancroft Diaries, 10 August 1863 (Connecticut Historical Society).

P. 19: *"Very very hot"*: Samuel F. Wells Day Book, 20 June 1868 (Pocumtuck Valley Memorial Association).

P. 19: *"hoed tobacco all day"*: Alden Briggs, Agricultural Diary, 26 July 1892 (Pocumtuck Valley Memorial Association)

P. 22: *"an expensive cigar"*: Kiernan, *Tobacco: A History*, 41–42.

P. 22: *arbiter of these matters*: Savona, "Made in the Shade"; Vaughan, "Wrapped Up."

P. 23: *"to grow Sumatra tobacco"*: *Country Gentleman* 67 (2 January 1902): 5.

P. 23: production statistics: Heimann, *Tobacco and Americans*, 110.

P. 23: *"hazardous experiment"*: Keach, in *Country Gentleman* 67 (8 May 1902): 388–89.

P. 24: Hartman Company: "The Hartman Tobacco Company Organized." Adolph and Samuel Hartman, pioneers in shade-grown tobacco, had begun business in Manchester, Connecticut, in 1882.

P. 24: acre statistics: Shade Growers Agricultural Association, *The Story of Tobacco Valley*, 15.

P. 24: *"It has been estimated*: Lang, "It's Hard Work, Mon."

P. 26: *"acres and acres of land"*: Savage, *Parrish*, 8.

TOBACCO PEOPLE

P. 29: Ebenezer Grant: Hosley, *Great River*, 84–85.

P. 30: *Yankee planter*: Billings, *Tobacco*, 311–16.

P. 31: George Trask: Ramsey, *History of Tobacco Production*, 150–53; Meta Lander, *Tobacco Problem*, xl.

P. 32: *"vegetable poison"*: Trask, *Letters on Tobacco*, 20–27.

P. 32: Arba Lankton: Lankton, *Incidents in the Life of Arba Lankton*.

P. 32: *"Tobacco fields and distilleries"*: Meta Lander, *The Tobacco Problem*, xvi.

P. 32: *"The use of tobacco"*: Arba Lankton's Total Abstinence and Anti-Tobacco Society, *Report of the Twelfth Year*, 1888.

P. 32: *"acts of religion"*: McCoubrey, *American Art*, 95–97.

P. 32: *"When, oh when"*: Trask, quoted from Meta Lander, *Tobacco Problem*, xvi.

P. 32: *"banks of the Connecticut"*: *Anti-Tobacco Journal* (November/December 1862).

P. 33: *"a kindly Providence"*: Twain, *Mark Twain's Letters, 1870–1871*, 275 (19 December 1870).

P. 33: *"the parent of American slavery"*: Robinson, *Facts for Farmers*, 953.

P. 33: *"loth to publish"*: "Hints for Tobacco Growing."

P. 33: *"Suggest this topic"*: French, "Morality of Tobacco Raising." For identification of Judge French, see Robinson, *Facts for Farmers*, 910.

P. 34: *"the use of tobacco"*: "Morality of Tobacco Raising."

P. 34: *nutritional crops*: "Tobacco Versus Useful Crops."

P. 34: *"good time for the growers"*: *American Agriculturalist* 26 (June 1867): 216–17.

P. 34: *"Some people have"*: Bagg, "Tobacco."

P. 35: *"Tobacco has risen"*: *Country Gentleman* 17 (November 1861): 346.

P. 35: *"unparalleled prosperity"*: "Tobacco Culture in the Connecticut Valley."

P. 35: *"tobacco fever"*: "Tobacco in Hampshire County."

P. 35: Hadley statistics: Klimm, *"Relation Between Certain Population Changes and the Physical Environment,"* 34.

P. 35: *"He lives in a pleasant"*: Thanet, "Farmer in the North."

P. 36: *"a Polander"*: Solomon Terry Wells Diaries, 8 March 1890 (Connecticut Historical Society).

P. 36: *"rocky farms of Connecticut"*: Ives. "Foreigner in New England."

P. 36: *"all our boys"*: Morse, "Earning a Valley."

P. 36: *"the quality of American citizenship"*: Schriftgiesser, *Gentleman from Massachusetts: Henry Cabot Lodge*, 115–16.

P. 37: *"a little nearer the slave trade"*: "Pole on the Farm and as a Citizen."

P. 37: *"Here under a New England sky"*: "Connecti-cut Valley Is Half Polish," published in 1927 by an unnamed newspaper. Clipping in the Polish folder in Special Collections, Jones Library, Amherst, Massachusetts.

P. 37: *heterogeneous community*: Siek, "Mobility and Success."

P. 37: *"possibly the most distinctive survival"*: Titus, "Pole in the Land of the Puritan."

P. 37: *"they add to agricultural resources"*: Barker, "How Poles Got Rich."

P. 38: *"the Polander in tobacco"*: Solomon Terry Wells Diaries, May 25, 1906, March 9, 1914 (Connecticut Historical Society) .

P. 38: *number of local farms*: Siek, "Mobility and Success."

P. 38: *One after another*: Fox, *Poles in America*, 75.

P. 38: *"allegiance to the land"*: Tyler, "Poles in the Connecticut Valley."

P. 39: *"flamboyant story"*: Jim Larkin Books, Crowley, Texas (via Bookfinder.com).

P. 40: Mr. and Mrs. Andrew Lyman: Eiseman and Janick, *In Touch with the Land*, n.p.

P. 40: *"Those leaves"*: Chase, *Journey to Boston*, 54.

P. 40: *"They were all nationalities"*: Henry Szydlo, oral history statement, 1982 (Thomas J. Dodd Research Center).

P. 41: *"as soon as you were big"*: Eiseman and Janick, *In Touch with the Land*.

P. 41: *One small farmer*: Brunet, "Crop Diversity Has Helped Wallace D. Hibbard."

P. 41: *"to survey and publicize"*: Trachtenberg, "Camera Work/Social Work," in *Reading American Photographs*, 200–201.

P. 41: *"The raising of tobacco"*: Hine, "Children and Tobacco in Connecticut."

P. 44: *African American population*: Schnip and Williamson, *Changing Landscape Through People*, n.p.

P. 44: *Not all their experiences were positive*: Tucker in *Agricultural History* 68 (Winter 1994): 68.

P. 44: *grade school education*: Ransom, "Jamaican Workers in the State of Connecticut."

P. 45: Amos Taylor; oral history statement, 1982 (Thomas J. Dodd Research Center).

P. 45: *The first arrivals*: Johnson, *Soldiers of the Soil*, 45–53.

TOBACCO SHEDS

P. 49: *"expression of site and climate"*: Moholy-Nagy, *Native Genius*, 44–45, 48.

P. 50: *Local traditions might indicate*: Hart and Mather, "The Character of Tobacco Barns."

P. 50: *transverse frame barn*: Nobel, *Wood, Brick, and Stone*, 11. A much rarer type is the balloon frame tobacco barn, for which see Killebrew and Myrick, *Tobacco Leaf*, Fig. 53.

P. 51: *"making the capacity"*: Phinney, "Up on the Hill."

P. 51: *Four-acre shed*: Solomon Terry Wells Diaries, September 11, 1912 (Connecticut Historical Society).

P. 52: *one farmer's production*: George L. Cooley, Farm Records (microfilm, Special Collections, Jones Library).

P. 52: *"old tobacco shed"*: Josiah Allen Journal, August 7, 1871 (Pocumtuck Valley Memorial Association)

P. 53: *held in place by gravity*: Halsted and Powell, *Barn Plans and Outbuildings*, 372–76.

P. 54: *the slanting door*: Killebrew and Myrick, "Tobacco Barns and Sheds."

P. 54: *top-hinged vents*: Garner, *Principles and Practical Methods of Curing Tobacco*, 29.

P. 54: *It has been noted*: Barakat, "Tobaccuary," 231–32.

P. 54: *When the leaf is newly hung*: New England Farmer 21 (November 1869): 506.

P. 56: *According to a publication*: Pack and Junnila, *Principles of Curing Broadleaf and Havana Seed Tobaccos*.

P. 56: *"there are almost as many"*: Hickey, *Harvesting and Curing of New England Stalk-Cut Tobacco*.

P. 56: *"The curing of tobacco"*: "How Tobacco Is Grown and Prepared for Market."

P. 57: *"twenty-four hour watch"*: Oscar Reese family, oral history statement, 1982 (Thomas J. Dodd Research Center).

P. 57: *"at night"*: Savage, *Parrish*, 155.

P. 57: *"ye chamber"*: Sheldon, *History of Deerfield, Massachusetts*, 1: 254.

P. 58: *"in the barn or some other building"*: Deane, "Tobacco."

P. 58: *"separate building"*: White, "The Tobacco Barn."

P. 58: *"English barn"*: Nobel and Seymour, "Distribution of Barn Types."

P. 58: *two-page spread*: Billings, *Tobacco*, 406–7.

P. 60: *"built expressly to cure tobacco"*: "Culture of Tobacco."

P. 60: *leaking smoke into the air*: see Hart and Mather, "Character of Tobacco Barns," 278, and Aaron Bohrod's painting, *Unstringing Tobacco*, 1940s (Sotheby's auction catalogue of *American Paintings, Drawings and Sculpture*, Sale 7480, 24 May 2000, #170).

P. 60: *"carted to the tobacco sheds for hanging"*: Watson, "Tobacco in Connecticut."

P. 60: *"the next thing"*: "Tobacco in Hampshire County."

P. 61: Elisha Wells shed: Garrison, *Landscape and Material Culture in Franklin County*, 90–92.

P. 61: *"put up a good frame"*: "Tobacco Sheds: How They Should Be Built." For another early description see "How Tobacco Is Grown and Prepared for Market."

P. 62: *"common in the Connecticut Valley"*: "Hints on Tobacco Culture No. II."

P. 62: *similar but more detailed cuts*: American Agriculturalist, *Tobacco Culture*, 30–31.

P. 62: *barn books*: Shoppell, "Barns and Out-Houses."

P. 63: *"Growing tobacco"*: Emil Mulnite, oral history statement (Luddy/Taylor Connecticut Valley Tobacco Museum).

P. 63: *repairs to farm structures*: Charles Hoffmann Record Book (Connecticut Historical Society), Josiah Allen Journal (Pocumtuck Valley Memorial Association), and others.

P. 63: *"raisings"*: Julius Robbins Diary (Pocumtuck Valley Memorial Association).

P. 63: *"raise a tobacco shed"*: Solomon Terry Wells Diaries, 25 May, 28 June, 1906 (Connecticut History Society).

P. 63: *"drew logs"*: Alden Briggs Diary, August 1–September 1, 1892 (Pocumtuck Valley Memorial Association).

P. 64: *"cut the posts for the shead"*: George Blodgett Diary, August 2–September 17, 1893 (Windsor Historical Society).

P. 65: *A study of 102 surviving sheds*: Procter, "History of Connecticut Shade Tobacco in Massachusetts."

P. 65: *"build a substantial structure"*: Killebrew and Myrick, *Tobacco Leaf*, 202–4.

P. 65: *"Fathers Tobacco Barn"*: Charles Hoffmann Record Book, February 27, 1886 (Connecticut Historical Society).

P. 65: *"took the barns and the tobacco"*: Enoch Pelton, oral history statement, 1982 (Thomas J. Dodd Research Center).

P. 65: *"We were firing the shed"*: Chester Woodford, oral history statement," 1982 (Thomas J. Dodd Research Center).

P. 67: *"The day after the hurricane"*: Mary Clark Griffin, oral history statement (Luddy/Taylor Connecticut Valley Tobacco Museum).

P. 67: *lost his sheds*: Emile Mulnite, oral history statement, 1982 (Thomas J. Dodd Research Center).

P. 67: *"4 acre tobacco shed"*: Solomon Terry Wells Diary, September 11, 1912 (Connecticut Historical Society).

P. 67: *"Dennis Byron's house"*: Solomon Terry Wells Diary, December 14, 1898 (Connecticut Historical Society).

P. 67: *"A tobacco shed burned down"*: William C. Huntington, oral history statement (Luddy/Taylor Connecticut Valley Tobacco Museum).

P. 68: Henry Scott to Emil Weber: Luddy/Taylor Connecticut Valley Tobacco Museum.

P. 68: *A builder out of Glastonbury*: Luddy/Taylor Connecticut Valley Tobacco Museum.

P. 68: Frank Zera shed: Kenyon, "Small Tobacco Farm Building Big Shed."

P. 68: *"the best form of shed"*: Crafts, "Cultivation of Tobacco No. 5."

P. 68: *"the best barn was the cheapest"*: Garner, *Principles*, 27–30.

P. 70: *"back room"*: Josiah Allen Journal, November 12, 1867, December 15, 1870, November 16, 1871 (Pocumtuck Valley Memorial Association).

P. 70: *"A chimney rises"*: White, "Tobacco Barn." See also Visser, *Field Guide*, 187 92.

P. 73: *This feature appeared early*: "Cultivation of Tobacco" (1863).

P. 73: *"basement room"*: White, "Tobacco Barn."

P. 73: *"While they worked"*: Clark, "Tobacco and History."

"HOW BEAUTIFUL IS USE"

P. 75: *"Architecture concerns itself"*: Ruskin, *Seven Lamps of Architecture*, 16.

P. 75: *"bicycle shed is a building"*: Pevsner, *Outline of European Architecture*, 15.

P. 76: *"form ever follows function"*: Sullivan, "Tall

Office Building Artistically Considered," 208.
Although the phrase is popularly cited as "form
follows function," Sullivan actually wrote "form
ever follows function, and this is the law." The
statement occurs within a paean to forms in
nature.

P. 76: *architectural lessons in mechanical design*:
Greenough, "American Architecture," 62–63.

P. 76: *"how beautiful is use!"*: quoted in Lewis,
Frank Furness: Architecture and the Violent Mind, 123.

P. 76: *"possesses in the highest degree"*: Cram, Introduction, ii.

P. 77: *"as though they had been grouped"*: Charles
Augustus Murray, quoted in Brown, *Inventing New
England*, 34.

P. 77: *"I used to love to go"*: Mary Clark Griffin,
oral history statement (Luddy/Taylor Connecticut Valley Tobacco Museum).

P. 77: *"One never looks upon them"*: Chase, *Journey to
Boston*, 15.

P. 77: *"nestle in nature"*: Emerson, "Nature"
(1843), *Essays by Ralph Waldo Emerson*, 382.

P. 78: *"designed artifacts"*: Hubka, "Just Folks
Designing."

P. 78: *"the existence of a man-made object"*:
Schlereth, *Material Culture Studies in America*, 3.

THE WANING OF THE SHEDS

P. 80: *"Yes, it's growing buildings"*: Francis Mocklis,
oral history statement (Luddy/Taylor Connecticut Valley Tobacco Museum).

P. 81: *"its death at the hands"*: Morris, *William Morris, Artist, Writer, Socialist*, 157.

FURTHER READING

MANUSCRIPT MATERIALS
AND OTHER SOURCES
**Agricultural Diaries, Account
Books, Etc.**

William B. Adams. "Diary," 1870–1908.
Described but unlocated in Pabst, *Agricultural
Trends*, 114–17.

Josiah Allen. Journal, 1861–95. Pocumtuck Valley Memorial Association, Deerfield, Mass.

Richard Catlin Arms. Account Books, 1862–70,
1870–92. Pocumtuck Valley Memorial Association, Deerfield, Mass.

James Bancroft. Diaries, 1855–80 (Bancroft Family Papers, 1801–1951). Connecticut Historical Society.

George A. Blodgett. Diary and Account Book,
July 1893–May 1894. Windsor (Connecticut)
Historical Society.

Alden B. Briggs. Agricultural Diary, 1889–98.
Pocumtuck Valley Memorial Association,
Deerfield, Mass.

George L. Cooley. "Tobacco Record," 1865–85.
Jones Library, Amherst Massachusetts.

Alice Gordon Higginson Fuller. Diary,
1855–1924 (55 volumes). Pocumtuck Valley
Memorial Association, Deerfield, Massachusetts.

Charles Hoffmann. Record Book, 1885–86. Connecticut Historical Society.

Rowland Nicholas. Account Book and Daybook,
1826–60. Pocumtuck Valley Memorial Association, Deerfield Mass.

Julius C. Robbins. Diary, 1840–82. Pocumtuck
Valley Memorial Association, Deerfield, Mass.

Samuel F. Wells. Day Book, 1868–73. Pocumtuck Valley Memorial Association, Deerfield,
Mass.

Solomon Terry Wells. Diaries, 1854–1914. Connecticut Historical Society.

Franklin H. Williams. Diary, 1852–91. Pocumtuck Valley Memorial Association, Deerfield
Mass.

John Wilson. Papers, 1850s onward. See Garrison, *Landscape and Material Culture*, Chapter 3.

Horace Wolcott. Account Book, 1842–48. Connecticut Historical Society.

Oral Histories

In the Archives of the Luddy/Taylor Connecticut Valley Tobacco Museum, Windsor, Connecticut:

Emil Mulnite (Broad Brook), William C. Huntington (Windsor), Stanley Waldron (South Windsor), Mary Clark Griffin (Windsor), and Francis Mocklis (Windsor). All given in 1995.

At the Thomas J. Dodd Research Center, University of Connecticut, Storrs, "Changing Landscape Through People: Connecticut Valley Tobacco":

Jan Carville, Bill Dunn, Emil Mulnite, Enoch Pelton, Stanley Waldron, James Farrell and Mrs. J. E. Sheperd, Ralph Holcombe, Richard Newfield, Wentworth Phillips, Oscar Reese Family, L. Ellsworth Stoughton, Henry Szydlo, Amos Taylor, Chester Woodford, and Don Woronecky. All recorded 1981–82.

PUBLICATIONS, DISSERTATIONS, AND OTHER SOURCES

Alcorn, Robert Hayden. *The Biography of a Town: Suffield Connecticut, 1670–1970*, Suffield: Connecticut Printers, 1970.

Allen, Frances Newton Symmes. *The Invaders*. Boston: Houghton Mifflin, 1913.

American Agriculturalist. *Tobacco Culture: Practical details from the selection and preparation of the seed and the soil, to harvesting, curing and marketing the crop*. New York: Orange Judd, ca. 1863.

Anderson, Paul J. *Tobacco Culture in Connecticut*. Bulletin 364. New Haven: Connecticut Agricultural Experiment Station, 1934.

Arthur, Eric Ross and Dudley Witney. *The Barn: A Vanishing Landmark in North America*. Greenwich, Conn.: New York Graphic Society, 1972.

Bacon, Edwin M. *The Connecticut River and the Valley of the Connecticut*. New York: G.P. Putnam's Sons, 1906.

Baer, Willis Nissley. *The Economic Development of the Cigar Industry in the United States*, Lancaster, Pa.: Art Printing Co., 1933.

Bagg, James Newton. "Tobacco." *New England Farmer* 10 (February 1858): 86.

Bain, George W. and Howard A. Meyerhoff. *The Flow of Time in the Connecticut Valley: Geological Imprints*. Springfield, Mass.: Connecticut Valley Historical Museum and Pratt Museum, 1963.

Baird, Theodore. *The Most of It: Essays on Language and the Imagination*. Ed. William H. Pritchard. Amherst, Mass.: Amherst College Press, 1999.

Balch, Emily Greene. *Our Slavic Fellow Citizens*. New York: Charities Publication Committee, 1910. Reprint 1983.

Barakat, Robert Abraham. "New England Tobacco Barns." Paper on file, Flynt Library, Historic Deerfield, Inc.

Barakat, Robert Abraham. "Tobaccuary: A Study of Tobacco Curing Sheds in Southeastern

Pennsylvania." Ph.D. dissertation, University of Pennsylvania, 1972.

Barker, Albert D. "How Poles Get Rich on N.E. Farms Where Yankees Fail." *Boston Sunday Herald*, May 4, 1924, 9.

"Barns, Not Bill-Boards." *New England Tobacco Grower* 5 (July 1904): 8.

Bell, Michael. *The Face of Connecticut: People, Geology, and the Land.* State Geological and Natural History Survey of Connecticut Bulletin 110. Hartford: Department of Environmental Protection, 1985.

Billings, E. R. *Tobacco: Its History, Varieties, Culture, Manufacture, and Commerce, with an Account of Its Various Modes of Use, from Its First Discovery Until Now.* Hartford: American Publishing Company, 1875. Reprint Wilmington, Del.: Scholarly Resources, 1973.

Brooks, Jerome E. *The Mighty Leaf: Tobacco Through the Centuries.* Boston: Little, Brown, 1952.

Brown, Dona. *Inventing New England: Regional Tourism in the Nineteenth Century.* Washington, D.C.: Smithsonian Institution Press, 1995.

Brunet, Kathleen. "Crop Diversity Has Helped Wallace D. Hibbard." *Amherst Bulletin*, September 7, 1988, Section 2.

Brunet, Kathleen. "'Smoke More Cigars' Was the Motto." *Amherst Bulletin*, September 7, 1988, Section 2.

Cabrera Infante, G. *Holy Smoke.* London: Faber and Faber, 1985.

Callahan, Patrick J. "Tobacco Farming Was Part of the Fabric of Life." *Amherst Bulletin*, 7 September 1988, Section 2.

Cane, Ena M. *Whately, 1771–1971: A New England Portrait*, Northampton, Mass.: Printed for the Town of Whately by Gazette Printing Co., 1972.

Chase, Mary Ellen. *A Journey to Boston.* New York: W.W. Norton, 1965.

Clark, Bert. "Tobacco and History." *Public Post* (Glastonbury, Connecticut, Historical Society) (April 24, 1967): 4.

Clark, Christopher Frederic. "Household, Market, and Capital: The Process of Economic Change in the Connecticut Valley of Massachusetts, 1800–1860." Ph.D. dissertation, Harvard University, 1982.

Clark, Christopher. *The Roots of Rural Capitalism. Western Massachusetts, 1780–1860.* Ithaca, N.Y.: Cornell University Press, 1990.

Cole, Thomas. "Essay on American Scenery." *American Monthly Magazine* 1 (January 1836): 1–12. Reprinted in John W. McCoubrey, ed., *American Art, 1700–1960: Sources and Documents.* Englewood Cliffs, N.J.: Prentice-Hall, 1965.

Crafts, J. M. "Cultivation of Tobacco No. 5." *Country Gentleman* 23 (31 March 1864): 203.

Crafts, James Monroe. *History of the Town of Whately, Mass.: Including a Narrative of Leading Events from the First Planting of Hatfield, 1661–1899.* Boston: New England Historic Genealogical Society, 1998. Revised and enlarged from Temple. *History of the Town of Whately*.

Cram, Ralph Adams. Introduction to P. H. Ditchfield, *Picturesque English Cottages and Their Doorway Gardens*. Philadelphia: J.C. Winston, 1905.

Crane, Charles Edward, Marion Hooper, Lewis Brown, Ralph Day, Newell Green, R. D. Snively, M. E. Snively, and Cortlandt Luce. *Life Along the Connecticut River*. Brattleboro, Vt.: Stephen Daye Press, 1939.

"Cultivation of Tobacco." *American Agriculturist* 22 (September 1863): 267.

"Cultivation of Tobacco." *American Agriculturalist* 33 (April 1874): 139.

"Culture of Tobacco" (and related titles). *American Agriculturist* 4 (April 1845): 19; 7 (March 1848): 101; (October 1848): 305; 10 (January 1851): 34; 11 (January 1854): 316; 16 (March 1857): 54–55.

"Culture of Tobacco." *Cultivator* 8 (June 1841): 100.

"Culture of Tobacco," *Cultivator* n.s. 8 (November 1860): 338–40.

"Culture of Tobacco," *Country Gentleman* 26 (September 1865): 203.

Curtis, Verna Posever and Stanley Mallach. *Photography and Reform: Lewis Hine & the National Child Labor Committee*. Milwaukee: Milwaukee Art Museum, 1984.

Deane, Samuel. "Tobacco." In Deane, *The New-England Farmer; or Georgical Dictionary*. Boston: Wells and Lilly, 1822. 456–58.

Delaney, Edmund T. *The Connecticut River: New England's Historic Waterway*. Chester, Conn.: Globe Pequot Press, 1983.

Delano, Jack. *Photographic Memories*. Washington, D.C.: Smithsonian Institution Press, 1997.

Dwight, Timothy. *Travels in New England and New York*. New Haven, Conn.: S. Converse, 1821–22. Reprint, ed. Barbara Miller Solomon. Cambridge, Mass.: Harvard University Press, 1969.

Edwards, Frances M. "Tobacco." *Connecticut Antiquarian* 9 (July 1951): 15–19.

Eiseman, Alberta and Dr. Herbert F. Janick, Jr. *In Touch with the Land: Images of Connecticut Farm Life, 1937–1985*. Hartford: Connecticut State Library, 1985.

Emerson, Ralph Waldo. *Essays by Ralph Waldo Emerson*. Intro. Irwin Edman. New York: Crowell, 1951.

Esty, Annette. *The Proud House*. New York: Harper, 1932.

Fairholt, Frederick W. *Tobacco: Its History and Associations*. London: Chatto and Windus, 1876.

Ferber, Edna. *American Beauty*. New York: Doubleday, 1931.

Field, Gregory. "Agricultural Science and the Rise and Decline of Tobacco Agriculture in the Connecticut River Valley." *Historical Journal of Massachusetts* 19 (Summer 1991): 155–74.

Foster, John H. *Agricultural Change in the Connecticut Valley Region of Massachusetts*. Amherst: Cooperative Extension Service, University of Massachusetts, 1955.

Fox, Paul. *The Poles in America*. New York: George H. Doran, 1922.

Foxe, Keith J. "Shade Tobacco Days." *CigarLife: The Internet Cigar Magazine*, 1999.

French, Judge [Henry Flagg]. "Morality of Tobacco Raising." *Cultivator* 12 (October 1864): 314–15.

Garner, W. W. *Principles and Practical Methods of Curing Tobacco*. Washington, D.C.: U.S. Government Printing Office, 1909.

Garrison, J. Ritchie. *Landscape and Material Culture in Franklin County, Massachusetts, 1770–1860*. Knoxville: University of Tennessee Press, 1991.

Gilbert, Edith. "Raising Tobacco in the Housatonic Valley," *Bulletin of the Connecticut League of Historical Studies* 23 (May 1973): 36–38.

Glassie, Henry H. "The Variation of Concepts Within Tradition: Barn Building in Otsego County, New York." In H. J. Walker and William George Haag, eds., *Man and Cultural Heritage: Papers in Honor of Fred B. Kniffen*. Baton Rouge: School of Geoscience, Louisiana State University, 1974.

Glassie, Henry H. *Vernacular Architecture*, Bloomington: University of Indiana Press, 2000.

Gordon, Ralph. "Profits Climb for Tobacco, But Barns Are Scarce." *[Springfield?] Sunday Republican* (April 13, 1991), A1, A16.

[Granby Public Library]. *Tobacco in Connecticut*. A series of bulletins and circulars published by the Connecticut Agricultural Experiment Station, New Haven, and the Storrs Agricultural Experiment Station, College of Agriculture, University of Connecticut, 14 bulletins and 2 circulars, various dates.

Greenough, Horatio. "American Architecture." 1843. Reprinted in *Form and Function: Remarks on Art, Design, and Architecture*, ed. Harold A. Small. Berkeley: University of California Press, 1957.

Griffin, Fred. "Tobacco Valley." *Connecticut Magazine* 1 (June 1935): 15–31.

Halley, Anne and Alan Trachtenberg. *Jerome Liebling Photographs*. Amherst: University of Massachusetts Press, 1982.

Halsted, Byron David and E. C. Powell. *Barn Plans and Outbuildings*. New and revised edition. New York: Orange Judd, 1906.

Hart, John Fraser. *The Rural Landscape*. Baltimore: Johns Hopkins University Press, 1998.

Hart, John Fraser and Eugene Cotton Mather. "The Character of Tobacco Barns and Their Role in the Tobacco Economy of the United States." *Annals of the Association of American Geographers* 51 (September 1961): 274–93.

Hartman Company. "The Hartman Tobacco Company Organized." *Tobacco Leaf* 64 (March 17, 1928): 6–7.

Heimann, Robert K. *Tobacco and Americans*. New York: McGraw-Hill, 1960.

Hendrickson, Clarence Irving. *An Economic Study of the Agriculture of the Connecticut Valley*. Vol. 4,

A History of Tobacco Production in New England. Bulletin 174. Storrs, Conn.: Storrs Agricultural Experiment Station, October 1931.

Hickey, L. P. M. *The Harvesting and Curing of New England Stalk-Cut Tobacco.* Hartford: Connecticut Valley Tobacco Association, 1923.

Hildebrand, Muriel. "Connecticut's Premier Cash Crop: Tobacco." *Bulletin of the Connecticut League of Historical Studies* 27 (March 1975): 7–9.

Hine, Lewis W. "Children and Tobacco in Connecticut." Report to the National Child Labor Committee, August 1917. National Child Labor Committee papers, Library of Congress, Manuscript Division.

"Hints for Tobacco Growing." *American Agriculturalist* 16 (March 1857): 54–55.

"Hints on Tobacco Culture No. II." *American Agriculturist* 21 (April 1862): 104.

Hoppin, Martha J. *Arcadian Vales: Views of the Connecticut River Valley.* Exhibition catalog. Springfield, Mass.: Springfield Library and Museums Association for George Walter Vincent Smith Art Museum, 1982.

Hosley, William N., ed. *The Great River: Art and Society of the Connecticut Valley, 1635–1820.* Hartford: Wadsworth Atheneum, 1985.

"How Tobacco Is Grown and Prepared for Market." *American Agriculturalist* 19 (March 1860): 78.

"How to Raise Tobacco." In American Agriculturalist, *Tobacco Culture: Practical Details from the Selection and Preparation of the Seed and the Soil, to Harvesting, Curing and Marketing the Crop.* New York: Orange Judd, ca. 1863. 30–31.

Howes, Alvah, George Howes, and Walter Howes. *New England Reflections, 1882–1907: Photographs by the Howes Brothers.* Ed. Alan B. Newman. New York: Pantheon Books, 1991.

Hubka, Thomas. "Just Folks Designing: Vernacular Designers and the Generation of Form." In Dell Upton and John Michael Vlach, eds., *Common Places: Readings in American Vernacular Architecture.* Athens: University of Georgia Press, 1986. 426–32.

Hubbard, Arthur W., Ruth C. Warner, Benjamin J. Toczydlowski, and Fred C. Warner. *History of the Town of Sunderland, Massachusetts, 1899–1954.* Vol. 2. Orange, Mass.: Art Press, 1954.

Imperial Agricultural Corporation. *Tobacco-Land in Old New England: How Yankee Ingenuity Defied Nature, Brought Tropical Climate to Connecticut, Created an Agricultural Business in a Great Industrial Area.* New York: Imperial Agricultural Corporation, 1945.

Ives, Rev. Joel S. "The Foreigner in New England." *Connecticut Magazine* 9 (1905): 245 ff.

Jacobstein, Meyer. *The Tobacco Industry in the United States.* New York: Columbia University Press, 1907. Reprint New York: Columbia University Press, 1968.

Johnson, Fay Clarke. *Soldiers of the Soil.* New York: Vantage Press, 1995.

Jorgensen, Neil. *A Guide to New England's Land-scape*. Chester, Conn.: Pequot Press, 1977.

Katra, Joseph. "A Survey of Polish Population of Northampton, 1889–1953." Unpublished paper, Amherst College, 1953.

Keach, S. B. "The Connecticut Tobacco Crop." *Cultivator and Country Gentleman* 59 (December 1894): 371–72.

Keach, S. B. Letter. *Country Gentleman* 67 (8 May 1902): 388–89.

Kelley, James B. "Research Problems in the Design of Tobacco Barns." *Agricultural Engineering* 5, (April 1924): 88–90.

Kenyon, Ted. "Small Tobacco Farm Building Big Shed." *Hartford Journal Inquirer*, 11 August 1997, 12.

Killebrew, J. B. and Herbert Myrick. "Tobacco Barns and Sheds." Chapter 9 in *Tobacco Leaf: Its Culture and Cure, Marketing and Manufacture*. New York: Orange Judd, 1897.

Kiernan, V. G. *Tobacco: A History*. London: Hutchinson Radius, 1991.

Klimm, Lester Earl. "The Relation Between Certain Population Changes and the Physical Environment in Hampden, Hampshire, and Franklin Counties, Massachusetts, 1790–1925." Ph.D. dissertation, University of Pennsylvania, 1933.

Lander, Meta [Margaret Woods Lawrence]. *The Tobacco Problem*. 5th ed. Boston: Lee and Shepard, 1885.

Lang, Joel. "It's Hard Work, Mon." *Northeast Magazine* (*Hartford Courant*), November 19, 1989, 10–14, 16–18, 26, 28–32.

Lankton, Arba. *Incidents in the Life of Arba Lankton, with Sermons and Lectures on Religion, Temperance and Anti-Tobacco*. Hartford, Conn.: Arba Lankton's Total Abstinence and Anti-Tobacco Society, 1891.

Lankton, Arba. *Arba Lankton's Total Abstinence and Anti-Tobacco Society*. Annual Reports. Hartford, Conn.: the Society, 1877 et seq.

Lewis, Michael J. *Frank Furness: Architecture and the Violent Mind*. New York: Norton, 2001.

Lewis, Thomas R. "The Landscape and Environment of the Connecticut River Valley." In William N. Hosley, ed., *The Great River: Art and Society of the Connecticut Valley, 1635–1820*. Hartford, Conn.: Wadsworth Atheneum, 1985. 3–14.

Lewis, Thomas R. *Near the Long Tidal River: Readings in the Historical Geography of Central Connecticut*. Washington, D.C.: University Press of America, 1981.

Lewis, Thomas R. "Recent Changes in the Connecticut Valley Tobacco Industry." *Journal of Geography* 68 (January 1969): 46–49. Reprinted in Lewis, *Near the Long Tidal River*.

Love, Aileen. "Frances Newton Symmes Allen. Her Life and Written Works." 1995. Paper on file, Flynt Library. Historic Deerfield, Inc.,

Loveland, A. L. "Tobacco in Connecticut." *Cultivator & Country Gentleman* 42 (August 1877): 551.

Lucey, Alexander A., Jr. "The Immigration of

Slavic Farmers to Hadley." MS thesis, Massachusetts State College, Amherst, 1936. Copy in Special Collections, Jones Library, Amherst.

McDonald, Adrian Francis. *The History of Tobacco Production in Connecticut*. New Haven, Conn.: Published for the Tercentenary Commission by Yale University Press, 1936.

Milkofsky, Brenda. "Connecticut Tobacco Farming." *Bulletin of the League of Historical Societies* 40 (July 1988): 6–10.

Miller, William J. *The Geological History of the Connecticut Valley of Massachusetts: A Popular Account of Its Rocks and Origin*. Northampton, Mass.: Hampshire Bookshop, 1921.

Moholy-Nagy, Sibyl. *Native Genius in Anonymous Architecture in North America*. New York: Horizon Press, 1957.

"Morality of Raising Tobacco." *Country Gentleman* 23 (October 1864): 274–75.

Morris, May. *William Morris, Artist, Writer, Socialist*. Oxford: Blackwell, 1936.

Morse, W. N. "Earning a Valley." *Outlook*, 10 September 1910, 80–86.

"New England." "Morality of Tobacco-Raising." *Country Gentleman and Cultivator* 13 (27 October 1864): 274–75.

Nobel, Allen G. *Wood, Brick, and Stone: The North American Settlement Landscape*. Vol. 2, *Barns and Farm Structures*. Amherst: University of Massachusetts Press, 1984.

Nobel, Allen G. and Gayle A. Seymour, "The Distribution of Barn Types in Northeastern United States." *Geographical Review* 72 (1982): 155–70.

O'Gorman, James F., ed. *Cervin Robinson: Photographs, 1958–1983*. Wellesley, Mass.: Wellesley College, 1983.

Pabst, Margaret Richards. *Agricultural Trends in the Connecticut Valley Region of Massachusetts, 1800–1900*. Smith College Studies in History 26 (1–4). Northampton Mass.: Department of History, Smith College, 1940–41.

Pack, A. Boyd and William A. Junnila. *Principles of Curing Broadleaf and Havana Seed Tobaccos*. New Haven: Connecticut Agricultural Experiment Station, July 1952.

Pevsner, Nikolaus. *An Outline of European Architecture*. 7th ed. Harmondsworth: Penguin Books, 1972.

Phinney, William R. "Up on the Hill." Typescript, 1956–57 (copy in the Jones Library, Amherst, Mass.). About the Allis family, farmers of Whately, and especially Irving Allis (1849–1929).

Piccin, Nancy. "Long Road Ahead for Saving Now-Vacant Tobacco Sheds." *Daily Hampshire Gazette*, August 9, 1988. Typical of the many articles on the subject published by local newspapers in recent years.

Pinsky, David. *Shade Grown Tobacco in Tobacco Valley: Its Economics and Manpower*. Storrs, Conn.: Labor Education Center, University of Connecticut, 1976.

"The Polanders in the Valley." *Daily Hampshire Gazette*, July 1, 1902.

"The Pole on the Farm and as a Citizen." *Daily Hampshire Gazette*, March 13, 1911.

Procter, Prudence. "A History of Connecticut Shade Tobacco in Massachusetts, and a Topology of Extant Tobacco Barns Based on a Survey Taken in Deerfield, Wapping and South Deerfield, Massachusetts." 1979. Paper on file, Flynt Library, Historic Deerfield, Inc.

Provost, Mal. "For Ed Kelley, Farming Is Always a Family Affair." *Amherst Bulletin*, September 7, 1988, Section 2.

Provost, Mal. "Tobacco: Pride of the Connecticut Valley." *Amherst Bulletin*, September 7, 1988, Section 2.

Prude, Jonathan. *The Coming of Industrial Order: Town and Factory Life in Rural Massachusetts, 1810–1860*. Amherst: University of Massachusetts Press, 1983.

Ramsey, Elizabeth. *The History of Tobacco Production in the Connecticut Valley*. Smith College Studies in History 15 (3–4). Northampton, Mass.: Department of History, Smith College, 1930.

Ransom, Reverdy C., III. "Jamaican Workers in the State of Connecticut." *Journal of Negro Education* 15 (Autumn, 1946): 717–21.

Rosenberg, John S. "Shade-Tobacco Growers Face Uncertain Future." *New York Times*, 1 June 1980, p. D1. Typical of newspaper articles of the period.

Ruskin, John. *The Seven Lamps of Architecture*. New York: Farrar, Straus, Giroux, 1979.

Russell, Howard S. *A Long Deep Furrow: Three Centuries of Farming in New England*, Hanover, N.H.: University Press of New England, 1976.

Savage, Mildred. *Parrish*. New York: Simon and Schuster, 1958. Also *Parrish*. Warner Brothers, 1961. Dir. Delmer Davies.

Savona, David. "Made in the Shade." *Cigar Aficionado* (December 1999): 266–77.

Savulis, Ellen, Lee Ann Beauchamp, Shelley Hight, Robert Painter, and Hugh Davis. "The Impact of the Decline in Tobacco Production on Cultural Resources in the Connecticut Valley." University of Massachusetts for the Massachusetts Historical Commission, 1984.

Schlereth, Thomas J. *Material Culture Studies in America*. Walnut Creek, Calif.: AltaMira Press, 1999

Schnip, Anabel and Katya Williamson. *Changing Landscape Through People: Connecticut Valley Tobacco*. Exhibition catalog. East Hartford: Edward E. King Museum of Aviation and Tobacco, 1982.

Schriftgiesser, Karl. *The Gentleman from Massachusetts: Henry Cabot Lodge*. Boston: Little, Brown, 1944.

Shade Growers Agricultural Association. *The Story of Tobacco Valley*. Hartford, Conn.: Shade Growers Agricultural Association, 1958.

Sheldon, George. *A History of Deerfield, Massachusetts: The Times When and the People by Whom It Was Settled, Unsettled and Resettled*. 2 vols. Deerfield, Mass.: E.A. Hall, 1895–96.

"Shingle Roofs." *New England Tobacco Grower* 5 (July 1904): 8.

Shoppell, Robert W. "Barns and Out-Houses." In *How to Build, Furnish and Decorate Consisting of Elevations and Plans for Houses, Barns, and Every Description of Outbuilding*. New York: Co-Operative Building Plan Association, 1883.

Sieger, Kelly. "A Southern Crop That Grew Up North." *Amherst Bulletin*, 7 September 1988, Section 2.

Siek, Anna Grazyna. "Mobility and Success: The Case of Selected Polish Immigrants and Their Descendants in Northampton, Massachusetts." Undergraduate thesis, Smith College, 1976. Copy in Special Collections, Jones Library, Amherst, Massachusetts.

Simeti, Mary Taylor. *On Persephone's Island: A Sicilian Journal*. New York: Knopf, 1986.

Soclof, Richard. "Preserving the Tobacco Barns of the Connecticut River Valley: Preserving an Era." Unpublished paper on deposit at the Luddy/Taylor Connecticut Valley Tobacco Museum.

Stewart, John Bailey. *The Production of Cigar-Wrapper Tobacco Under Shade in the Connecticut Valley*. Washington, D.C.: U.S. Government Printing Office, 1908.

Stoughton, James Alden. *A Corner Stone of Colonial Commerce*. Boston: Little Brown, 1911.

Sullivan, Louis H. "The Tall Office Building Artistically Considered." In *Kindergarten Chats and Other Writings*. New York: Wittenborn, 1947.

Temple, J. H. *History of the Town of Whately, Mass. including a narrative of leading events from the first planting of Hatfield: 1660-1871*. Boston: Printed for the town by T. R. Marvin & Son, 1872.

Thanet, Octave. "The Farmer in the North." *Scribner's* 15 (January–June 1894): 323–30.

Thomson, Betty Flanders. *The Changing Face of New England*. New York: Macmillan, 1958. Reprint Boston: Houghton Mifflin, 1977.

Tilley, Nannie M. *The Bright-Tobacco Industry, 1860–1929*. New York: Arno Press, 1972.

Titus, Edward Kirk. "The Pole in the Land of the Puritan." *New England Magazine* 29 (October 1903): 162–66.

"Tobacco—Its History, Cultivation, and Profits of Production." In Solon Robinson, ed., *Facts for Farmers; Also for the Family Circle*. 2 vols. New York: A. J. Johnson, 1869. 2: 953–64.

"Tobacco Culture in the Connecticut Valley." *Springfield Daily Republican*, November 21, 1873, 5–6.

"Tobacco Culture—The Harvest." *American Agriculturist* 31 (October 1872): 372–73.

"Tobacco in the Connecticut Valley—Special Crops." *American Agriculturalist* (September 1874): 338–39.

"Tobacco in Hampshire County." *New England Farmer* 15 (November 1863): 358–59.

Tobacco Institute. *Connecticut and Tobacco: A Chapter in America's Industrial Growth*, Washington, D.C.: Tobacco Institute, 1972.

"Tobacco Shed." *American Agriculturist* 19 (March 1860): 78.

"Tobacco Sheds: How They Should Be Built." *Homestead* 2 (March 5, 1857): 380. See also 3 September 1857, 796.

"Tobacco Versus Useful Crops."*New England Farmer* 11 (November 1859): 531–33.

Trachtenberg, Alan. *Reading American Photographs: Images as History, Matthew Brady to Walker Evans.* New York: Hill and Wang, 1989.

Trask, George. *Letters on Tobacco, for American Lads; or Uncle Toby's Anti-Tobacco Advice to His Nephew Billy Bruce.* Fitchburg Mass.: the author, 1860. One of Trask's "Anti-Tobacco Tracts for Youth."

[Trask, George, ed.] *Anti-Tobacco Journal.* Boston, 1859–62.

Trask, George. *Tobacco Crop a Curse to the Connecticut Valley.* Fitchburg Mass.: Anti-Tobacco Tract Depository, ca. 1865.

Twain, Mark. *Mark Twain's Letters.* Vol. 4, *1870–1871.* Ed. Victor Fischer and Michael B. Frank. Berkeley: University of California Press, 1995.

Tyler, Elizabeth Stearns. "The Poles in the Connecticut Valley." *Smith College Monthly* 16 (June 1909): 579–86.

Vaughan, Mark. "Wrapped Up: Some of the World's Best Cigars Use Connecticut Tobacco Wrapper Leaves." *Cigar Aficionado* (Winter 1992–93): 50–57, 121–23.

Visser, Thomas Durant. *Field Guide to New England Barns and Farm Buildings,* Hanover, N.H.: University Press of New England, 1997.

Vitruvius. *The Ten Books on Architecture.* Trans. Morris Hickey Morgan. New York: Dover, 1960.

Watson, Henry. "Tobacco in Connecticut." *Cultivator* 1 (1844): 89.

The Wedding Night. Samuel Goldwyn, 1935. Dir. King Vidor.

Wells, Daniel W. and Reuben F. Wells. *A History of Hatfield, Massachusetts, in Three Parts.* Springfield, Mass.: F.C.H. Gibbons, 1910.

Welles, Mary Crowell. *Child Laborers in the Shade Grown Tobacco Industry in Connecticut.* Hartford: Consumers' League of Connecticut, [1917].

White, W. H. "Hints on Tobacco Culture—VI." *Cultivator & Country Gentleman* 32 (July 1869): 52–53.

White, W. H. "Tobacco Barn." *American Farmer and Rural Register* (March 1874): 103.

White, W. H. "Tobacco Barn." *Country Gentleman* 29 (August 1867): 114.

White, W. H. "Tobacco—Its Culture." *Cultivator and Country Gentleman* 27 (February 1866): 73–74.

Wood, Joseph S. *The New England Village.* Baltimore: Johns Hopkins University Press, 1997.

Wright, Frank Lloyd. "The Sovereignty of the Individual." 1910. In *Writings and Buildings,* ed. Edgar Kaufmann and Ben Raeburn. Cleveland: World, 1967

INDEX

Page references in *italics* indicate illustrations.

ACKNOWLEDGMENTS

This publication was made possible by generous research grants from Wellesley College and Furthermore, the publication program of the J. M. Kaplan Fund.

The following have furthered my work in one way or another: Drew Alfgren (Kuhn Library, University of Maryland Baltimore County), Robert A. Barakat, John Latchford Beck (Kuhn Library, University of Maryland Baltimore County), James F. Bennett (Glastonbury Historical Society), David Bosse (Flynt Library, Historic Deerfield, Inc.), Richard Candee (Boston University), Robert and Mary Lou Cutter (Hatfield Historical Commission), Walter Czajkowski (Hadley, Massachusetts), Amber Degn (Windsor Historical Society), Jared Edwards (Hartford), Suzanne L. Flynt (Memorial Hall Museum, Deerfield), Ritchie Garrison (University of Delaware), Kenneth Hafertepe (Baylor University), Margo Jones Architects (Greenfield, Massachusetts), Jo Joslyn (University of Pennsylvania Press), Bruce Kirby (Manuscript Division, Library of Congress), Jan Kornbluth (Portland, Maine), Reginald McDaniel (South Carolina Tobacco Museum), Brian and Alice McGowan (Blue Meadow Farm, Montague, Massachusetts), Mary Alice Molloy (Chicago), Linda Muehlig (Smith College Museum of Art), Marion M. Neilson (Luddy/Taylor Connecticut Valley Tobacco Museum), Dennis E. McGrath (Minneapolis), Richard Newfield (former head of the Hartman Tobacco Company, Hartford), Norman, Florence, and Nancy Nobel (Suffield, Connecticut), Martha Noblick (Flynt Library, Historic Deerfield, Inc.), Walter K. "Skip" Rapp (former shed builder), Mildred Savage (Norwich, Connecticut), Daniel Smiarowski (Sunderland, Massachusetts), Robert T. Silliman (Windsor Historical Society), Laura Katz Smith (Thomas J. Dodd Research Center, University of Connecticut), Michael Steinitz (Massachusetts Historical Commission), Sandy Williams (Williams Farm, Deerfield, Massachusetts), and Gary Van Zante (Southeastern Architectural Archive, Tulane University).